I WAS *three years old, at my Grandparents' farm. It was Monday – washday. The washing was always done in a separate building, the wash house. As Granny was out doing the washing, I was in the kitchen with my Aunt Edith (a young teenager at that time). I kept pestering Edith to take me out to be with Granny. Edith kept telling me that I was a Big Girl and that I could go by myself. I was SURE that I was not big enough to go by myself, and I kept telling her that the Gander would get me. Edith did not believe for one moment that the Gander wanted anything to do with me. (Fine for her to say. It obviously did not flap its wings and hiss at her when she was out helping Granny feed the chickens!!!) There was a very funny feeling in my stomach. Something was telling me not to go, BUT Edith was so much bigger than me, and so much smarter, she must be right!!!*

O.K., out the door – down the steps – three steps toward the wash house. Out of nowhere hurtled the Gander!!! Wings a flapping, he tried to pick at my eyes!!! He knocked me down in the sand, but I grabbed his neck with my little hand and had enough sense to keep my skinny arm stiff and my head down – to keep him at arm's length, as well as trying to protect my eyes. Of course, I SCREAAAAAMED blue bloody murder. He was still able to grab the hair on my head and pull it out in bunches. He beat me with those powerful wings that felt like broom handles. My first bad experience in life.

Thankfully, people came from everywhere. I was rescued, my many bruises and welts were tended to. Through the haze of my tears I saw Grandpa chasing the Gander, who was now making a speedy exit, trying to get to the safety of the barn. Granny was hollering "Pa – don't kill it!!!" Well Grandpa caught it, and did the right thing, in my opinion – I'm sure he wrung its neck. I was spared the gory details. The next day we ate that Gander.

This episode taught me two things: 1. When your stomach warns you about something – listen to it. 2. With team work (and Grandpa on your team) – it is possible TO EAT THE ENEMY. But, shucks, it only worked the once !!!

(see the inside back cover for the illustrated conclusion to this story.)

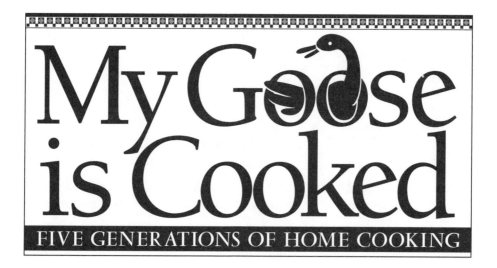

My Goose is Cooked

FIVE GENERATIONS OF HOME COOKING

ONEY MARTIN

PICTURED ON THE FRONT COVER:

Georgia Raised Biscuits, page 14

Sweet Potato & Pineapple Soufflé, page 78

Apple-Pork Stew, page 109

My Goose is Cooked — Five Generations of Home Cooking
by
ONEY MARTIN

First Printing – January 2002

**Copyright © 2002 by
Oney Martin**

**Published by
Marfac Industries Ltd.
38 Patterson Drive S.W., Calgary, Alberta, Canada T3H 2B7
Fax: (403) 242-7985   E-mail: oneym@telusplanet.net**

National Library of Canada Cataloguing in Publication Data

Martin, Iona, 1930-

My goose is cooked

Includes index.

ISBN 1-894022-70-X

1. Cookery, Canadian. 2. Frontier and pioneer life – Canada,
Western. I. Title.

TX715.6.M377 2002   641.5971   C2001-911738-8

Photography by
Ross (Hutch) Hutchinson, Hutchinson and Company

Cover and Page Design by
Brian Danchuk, Danchuk Design

Page formatting and index by Iona Glabus, PW Group

Designed, Printed and Produced in Canada by
**Centax Books, A Division of PW Group
Publishing Director, Photo Designer and Food Stylist – Margo Embury
1150 Eighth Avenue, Regina, Saskatchewan, Canada S4R 1C9**
(306) 525-2304   **Fax: (306) 757-2439**
centax@printwest. com   **www.centaxbooks.com**

Table of Contents

These recipes have been tested in U.S. standard measurements. Common metric measurements are given as a convenience for those who are more familiar with metric. These recipes have not been tested in metric.

DEAR FRIENDS,

ORIGINALLY my intent was to create a handbook for my three sons, who have of late become interested in cooking. There are phone calls daily, "What's in this?" or "How do you make that?" Now, the last thing in the world I want is for the phone calls to stop. I love them. However, being a realist, I know that these things should be written down for them for a later date. Like most things in life that start out simply, one thing builds to create another. I find myself having compiled hundreds of recipes from five generations, from my grandparents, parents, my own, my children and my grandchildren, as well as our many friends, a lot of simple, basic recipes. Some were old family favourites that had not been written down anywhere, which caused me to really think back and, at times, recreate. A lot of testing and retesting was involved.

Actually, the searching, and thinking made me realize how very hard the people that settled this country worked, your ancestors and mine. Life was a partnership of hard work. The men worked outside and the women worked inside (many worked outside also). There is an old saying, "Men may work from sun to sun – but women's work is never done." Do you suppose the pioneer women felt the truth in that statement? If they felt it, they would not have spoken it. These pioneer grandmothers will be remembered for the unique lives they led. Often leaving the security of their cultured homes and forging west to make their marks. They urged their communities to build schools, churches and hospitals, and made significant contributions toward civilizing the West. Let us not forget their faith and determination, which has become an important part of our heritage.

With all the kitchen devices and appliances that we now have, I wonder if a young person today can comprehend or relate to how difficult food preparation was when Western Canada was being settled. Let's think about it for a moment. There were no fridges, ice boxes maybe, but if you lived in the country, or in a small town, there was no ice delivery. No mixmaster, no blender, no food processor, no electric tea kettle, no electricity and, last but not least, no modern stove or microwave. Their stoves were temperamental wood/coal stoves, with an insatiable appetite for fuel, with the never-ending ashes that had to be dealt with. Water, hot or cold, did not come from a tap in the sink, but rather from a pump. If you were lucky it was in your kitchen sink, otherwise it was in the yard. If you lived in a small village, there was the town pump, blocks away.

Forget the corner supermarket with packaged meat and vegetables, if you were lucky the general store might be only 20 to 30 miles away. If you wanted milk, you had a cow that had to be milked twice a day, at its convenience. The milking of the cow and the separating of the milk was often the husband's department, but the washing of the milk separator, twice a day, was definitely a household job. It not only had to be washed and cleaned, but also sterilized, to keep bacteria from getting a start, and making the whole family sick. Twice a day!!!

Let's think for another moment of the work involved in preparing Sunday dinner (the day of rest.) If chicken was on the menu, Grandpa had to go out before the chickens were let out of the chicken coop, select a chicken and chop off the head. Granny, meanwhile, was getting the stove hot and getting water out of the well and onto the stove, in an enormous pot, to scald the chicken for easy feather removal. After the plucking came the evisceration, a job that would turn many modern cooks into vegetarians. Once the chicken was oven-ready, there was a trip to the garden (or root cellar, depending on the season): the potatoes must be dug up and cleaned; peas picked and shelled; corn picked and husked; onions pulled, washed and peeled, and brought back to the house. If there was enough time and energy left – dessert was whipped up. (No wonder a simple recipe like bread pudding was welcomed.) The point I am making is that these early settlers worked very hard – the men in the field – the women in the kitchen. Too often the work the women did is mentioned only in passing. Let us, you and I, take the time to salute those tireless pioneer women who worked from sunup to sundown. They tolerated much and complained little.

My mother's illness, when I was very young, required that my grandparents look after me for several years. A tremendous bond developed and now, years later, I look back with wonder at their eager spirits, abiding good nature and amazing accomplishments.

As you can appreciate, this has really been a trip back in time for me. I was about three years old when I fell in love with a crockery bowl and a wooden spoon. My Aunt Edith had just made a cake (chocolate) and hustled it into the oven in the coal stove. She then sat me down on the floor with the bowl and a teaspoon and taught me how to taste the "Good Stuff" that was left in the bowl. It was finger lickin' good, and I was hooked for life. My enthusiasm has never waned.

Granny's and Edith's influence on me was so strong that, in dealing with some of these recipes, I can still hear them saying, "Don't be stingy with the cream." "Make sure you beat that butter and sugar until it is pale yellow." "Don't be afraid to get your hands into it" (with pickles or fruitcake). They had me baking cakes alone when I was six (using that same crockery bowl and the wooden spoon). I used to think that my skinny arms would break, but I would not quit, nor ask for help. (At the time, I thought I was doing it on my own. I realize, now, that they were hovering over my shoulder. Like mother hens, they were keeping a close eye on my every move.)

As time went by, my arms grew stronger as did my interest in cooking. Growing up in Medicine Hat, a place that could truly have been the heart of the

United Nations, we had every nationality and culture, all with their own recipes and ways of doing things, I began to realize the rich diversity of food.

In our early married life, right after WW II, when we were a young family living in Medicine Hat, we were fortunate enough to have a lot of friends. None of us were poor, but no one had ten cents to waste. (Well, maybe by today's standards we were all poor.) Being young, with voracious appetites, food was always a topic of conversation. There was a lot of laughter that went along with the swapping of recipes. Most of the time it was a case of the same ingredients just put together in a different way. There must have been one hundred ways of taking a pound of hamburger, stretching it to feed four, and making it taste delicious. There were also an endless stream of flour and water, dough concoctions, which I have not bothered to record.

I would be remiss to not express the pleasure I have had in the research and compilation of this project. You have surely sensed that the gathering of all these recipes into one place has been a long, but enriching, sentimental journey, rewarding in a way that words will never really convey.

I wish to express a heartfelt appreciation to each and every member of my family, from my husband, Doug, to my boys Greg, Dan and Mike, and my grandchildren Tracey, Chris, Nikki and Amanda, for prodding me into creating this book. Thanks also to the many friends and relatives who have shared their recipes over the years. A special thanks to Wendy Hands for getting me started, and to Johanna Bates for seeing me over the rough spots and not allowing me to quit, and to Margo Embury for seeing me through to the finish.

Oney Martin

Breads,
Biscuits,
Muffins
&
Batters

PROCEDURES: Batters & Dough

The general methods for each of these remains consistent. Unlike soups or stews where you can vary ingredients and quantities, baking involves chemistry, so methods and quantities must be precise.

Muffin Method: Put all of the dry ingredients, i.e., flour, sugar, baking powder, in a bowl. Make a well in the middle of the dry ingredients and pour in the liquids, i.e., milk, eggs, melted butter or oil. Mix the batter just enough to incorporate all of the ingredients. Spoon into greased muffin cups.

Pancake Method: Same as muffins, except there is more liquid. Pancake batter is runny. You can pour it readily.

Cake Method: With an electric mixer, beat the butter until soft. Add sugar; beat until light and creamy. Add eggs; continue to beat until pale yellow and creamy. Add the liquids and the dry ingredients alternately, a little flour, a little milk, until you have used them all up. Continue to beat only until all ingredients are mixed in. Pour into prepared pan.

Cookie Method: This is the same as the cake method, except there is not a lot of liquid to add. The dough is much stiffer.

Angel or Sponge Cake Method: With an electric mixer, beat the egg whites until stiff. Combine flour and sugar and fold, 1 tbsp. (15 mL) at a time, into the beaten egg whites. Pour into an angel food cake pan - DO NOT GREASE the pan.

Pastry Method: Put flour, salt, sugar into a bowl or food processor. Cut in pieces of the cold shortening. Pulse in the food processor or use an electric mixer just until it becomes crumbly. Add ice water (by hand) and mix only enough to get the dough to form a ball. DO NOT OVERWORK. (The dough toughens up if overworked.)

Biscuit Method: This is the same as the pastry method, only you have a little more liquid.

Bread Method: Proof the yeast – which means to put it into the lukewarm water with a little sugar until it bubbles and foams (10 minutes). Add sugar, shortening, salt and water (or milk), plus half of the flour, and beat, with an electric mixer with a dough hook, until elastic/springy. This is called a sponge. Now, put the balance of the flour on the counter in a circle – make a well in the middle. Pour the sponge into the well and work the flour into the sponge, using the heel of your hand – this is called kneading. Knead the dough until it is no longer sticky and it springs back when you poke it. Place the dough in a large buttered bowl; let rise until it doubles in size – then punch down. Let it rise for a second time – punch down and make loaves. Place loaves in greased pans. Allow to rise again, until doubled in bulk. Pop into a 400°F (200°C) oven for ¾ hour. Brush tops of loaves with melted butter 5 minutes before you take them out of the oven. Turn loaves out of pans to cool on a rack.

Basic Bread & Bun Dough

2 tbsp. *(30 mL)* **yeast**
5 cups *(1.25 L)* **warm water**
½ cup *(125 mL)* **sugar**
½ cup *(125 mL)* **butter OR goose fat**
1 tbsp. *(15 mL)* **salt**
2 eggs, **beaten**
10-12 cups *(2.5-3 L)* **flour**

2 cups *(500 mL)* **flour for kneading**

Use a kneading pan or a very large crockery or stainless steel bowl, or an electric mixer with a dough hook.

Use the Bread Method on page 10. You will use all the flour, and may need a little more during the kneading process. Continue to knead and work flour in until it is no longer sticky.

Rub the kneading pan with oil or butter. Place dough in pan and rub with butter or oil; cover and let sit in warm place until doubled in bulk. Punch it down and let it rise again.

Divide the dough into 4 equal parts. To form into loaves about 5 x 9" (13 x 23 cm), pat the dough into rough rectangles; fold in the ends, then fold in the sides, pinching the seams together at the bottom. Put the shaped loaves into greased loaf pans; rub with a little butter or oil and let rise again.

Bake at 400°F (200°C) for 45 to 50 minutes*. Brush the crust with a little melted butter 5 minutes before you take the loaves out of the oven.

The same dough is used for buns. You could make 1 pan of buns and 3 loaves of bread. Bake the buns for 30 minutes.

Yield: 4 large loaves

*To test if loaves are done, rap the top of each loaf with your knuckles. When done, loaves will sound hollow.

No matter what else you serve – sumptuous or plain – it is the homemade bread that your family and friends will find irresistible. Compliments will abound. Trust me on this one!

SOME THINGS *in this life cannot be substituted. Making homemade bread is a good example. There has been nothing developed, from ancient times until now, that can turn a house into a home quicker than the heavenly, wafting aroma of freshly baked bread. Bread is the staff of life; different varieties are rooted in every culture on earth.*

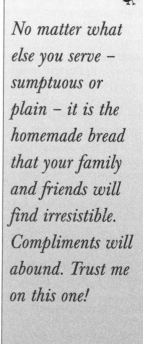

Kiechle/Küchle/Kuechle (keek-la)

One of Pauline Martin's specialties, this is a treat for bread-making day. As you can see by the various spellings, it has been popular in many regions of Germany.

¼ recipe of bread dough, page 11
oil for deep-frying

¾ cup *(175 mL)* granulated sugar
 OR icing (confectioners') sugar

OR

Cinnamon Sugar:
¾ cup *(175 mL)* sugar
½ tsp. *(2 mL)* cinnamon

OR

1 cup *(250 mL)* sour cream
½ garlic clove, minced

cookie tray lined with paper towel

Preheat deep-fat fryer to 365°F (185°C).

When bread dough has risen once, gently cut off as thin a piece as you can — about the size of a small saucer. Do not pat or roll as you want the air bubbles to remain in the dough.

Carefully drop the dough pieces into hot fat — brown on both sides. Remove the Kiechle, shake off excess oil, and place on a paper-lined tray.

Sprinkle the Kiechle with granulated or icing sugar or cinnamon sugar or, for a savory version, top with sour cream combined with minced garlic. Eat while hot.

Portions: 3 to 4 Kiechle per person

KIECHLE (keek-la) is a flat, deep-fried bread from Germany, much like yeast doughnuts or spudnuts. Every nationality under the sun has this recipe, in some form or another, all with different names and shapes. Basic bread dough is deep-fat-fried in saucer-sized pieces, sprinkled with sugar, sugar and cinnamon, honey or, if it is close to lunch time, it can also be spread with sour cream and garlic. It must be eaten hot and fresh! My grandchildren have always had this at the top of their list. We work as a team. I do the deep-fat frying, they sprinkle the sugar on the Kiechle as they are removed from the fat. A good system, but it is amazing how far the sugar manages to travel across the kitchen floor.

Cinnamon Buns

2 tbsp. *(30 mL)* yeast
5 cups *(1.25 L)* warm water
¾ cup *(175 mL)* sugar
¾ cup *(175 mL)* butter
1 tsp. *(15 mL)* salt
3 eggs, beaten
10-12 cups *(2.5-3 L)* white flour

4 cups *(1 L)* corn syrup
3 cups *(750 mL)* brown sugar
6 tsp. *(35 mL)* cinnamon
½ cup *(125 mL)* soft butter
2 cups *(500 mL)* flour for kneading

Prepare dough as in Basic Bread Method, page 10. Allow dough to rise. Prepare 2 pans, 13 x 18 x 1" (33 x 45 x 2.5 cm), by buttering them well. Spread half of the corn syrup in the bottom of each pan.

In a separate bowl, combine the brown sugar and cinnamon.

After the dough has risen once or twice, cut it in 2 equal pieces. With a rolling pin, on a floured surface, roll each piece into a rectangle about ½" (1.3 cm) thick.

Spread the dough evenly with butter – leaving 1" (2.5 cm) on the outside edge of the long side unbuttered. Brush that 1" (2.5 cm) with water. Sprinkle the brown sugar and cinnamon mixture over the buttered surface. Roll up from the side that has sugar to the very edge. Pinch the roll shut. The water-brushed edge helps seal the roll. Cut in 1" (2.5 cm) slices and place carefully in the prepared pan, cut side up. Let the buns rise until doubled in size.

Bake at 400°F (200°C) for 30 minutes, or until light brown. Watch carefully so they do not burn.

When you remove the rolls from the oven, let them sit for about 2 minutes (maximum) and then turn them out onto a piece of aluminum foil. Do not be stingy with the foil or you will have hot syrup all over the counter.

Yield: approximately 50 buns

The hard part here? Try not to eat too many as they come out of the oven.

IF AUNT EDITH had any sour cream in the fridge (real farm cream we are talking about here) she would pour it over the buns just before she put them in the oven. Now we are talking scrumptious!!!

Georgia Raised Biscuits

Georgia Raised Biscuits are special – light, fluffy and buttery.

1 tbsp. *(15 mL)* yeast
2 cups *(500 mL)* warm water
1 tbsp. *(15 mL)* sugar
1 tsp. *(5 mL)* salt
½ cup *(125 mL)* butter
4½ cups *(1.125 L)* flour

Place the yeast and water in a mixing bowl for about 10 minutes.

When the yeast is proofed, add the remaining ingredients, except for 2 cups (500 mL) of flour. With an electric mixer, beat the dough until it has a very elastic consistency, then slowly stir in the remaining flour. Knead well.

Divide the dough into 2 portions. Roll each out to ¼" (1 cm)*; cut with a 2" (5 cm) cutter. Spread each round with soft butter and stack them, 2 high, with butter between and on top.

Place the biscuits on a greased cookie sheet. Allow biscuits to rise until they have doubled in bulk.

Bake at 400°F (200°C) for 15 to 20 minutes.

Yield: approximately 26 to 30 biscuits

Pictured on the front cover.

* The dough will shrink – so allow it to shrink and then cut with a 2" (5 cm) cutter.

Bread dough is totally different from Pastry Dough. You can work it until the cows come home. The more you work it and the more elasticity it has (the more air holes) the better.

Irish Soda Bread

1½ cups *(375 mL)* white flour

1½ cups *(375 mL)* whole-wheat flour

1 tbsp. *(15 mL)* baking powder

1 tsp. *(5 mL)* baking soda

1 tsp. *(5 mL)* salt

2 tbsp. *(30 mL)* sugar

1 tsp. *(5 mL)* caraway seeds

1½ cups *(375 mL)* buttermilk OR sour milk

2 tbsp. *(30 mL)* butter, melted

In a large bowl, mix all the dry ingredients together. Add buttermilk and melted butter; mix thoroughly but do not overwork.

Pat the dough into an 8 or 9" (20 or 23 cm) pie plate – the dough should be about 1½" (4 cm) thick.

Mark the dough into quarters by cutting it about one-quarter through.

Bake at 375°F (190°C) for 40 minutes.

Brush the top of the loaf with butter. Serve hot.

Serves 8

Pictured on page 69.

This dense, heavy bread is best served immediately. It is perfect with soups and stews.

It was not until after Jimmie's passing that the family became aware of his recipe for Irish Soda Bread. It had been given to his very good friend Brian Ashwick many years ago. Brian translated it from pounds, ounces and pinches to cups and teaspoons.

Thank you Brian.

JIMMIE MARTIN, *my father-in-law, was born in Ireland and moved to Canada at the age of 15. Although he was very young when he moved, he remained totally Irish all his life. He even believed in leprechauns. Add to that his nervousness about the "wee ghosties" and you have a colourful, lovable character.*

His biggest fear in daily life was mice. When he initially came to this country he had taken a job on a farm helping with the harvest. One day, to his horror, a mouse ran up his pant leg. From that day on, anytime Jimmie had to work outside, in the garden, or mowing the lawn – he would stretch a rubber jar ring around the cuff of his pants to discourage another calamity. (He hoarded used rubber jar rings, and became very nervous when they became scarce during the war.) I heard the mouse story many times, but I laughed so hard that I never had enough sense to ask him how he actually got rid of the mouse. Do you suppose he had to drop his drawers? Knowing him, I doubt it. I suspect there was such a commotion that the mouse died of fright.

Brian's Beer Bread

Beer bread along with a bowl of homemade soup is called contentment. Try it "straight" or add your favourite herbs.

2¾ cups *(675 mL)* white flour
2 tbsp. *(30 mL)* sugar
2 tbsp. *(30 mL)* baking powder
1 tsp. *(5 mL)* salt
12 oz. *(341 mL)* can beer or ale
　　(I use Big Rock – Grasshopper or
　　Warthog)

Options:
¼ tsp. *(1 mL)* dried oregano
¼ tsp. *(1 mL)* dried sage
¼ tsp. *(1 mL)* dried thyme
¼ tsp. *(1 mL)* dried dillweed

In a large bowl, combine all of the dry ingredients. Add the herbs now, if using. Add the beer (room temperature).

Pour the batter into a sprayed 4 x 8" (10 x 20 cm) loaf pan.

Bake at 375°F (190°C) for 50 to 60 minutes.

After removing the loaf from the oven, brush the top of the loaf with melted butter. Allow it to cool in the pan for 10 minutes. Turn onto a rack. Serve warm.

Serves 6

Variation: For **Whole-Wheat Beer Bread**, 1 cup (250 mL) of whole-wheat flour may be substituted for 1 cup (250 mL) of the white flour.

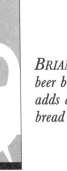

BRIAN ASHWICK, my father-in-law's good friend, shared this tangy beer bread recipe with me. The beer makes this bread rise well and it adds a yeasty flavour and aroma. Unlike the Irish Soda Bread, this bread lasts up to 2 days. It also makes very good toast.

Baking Powder Biscuits

2 cups *(500 mL)* flour
4 tsp. *(20 mL)* baking powder
½ tsp. *(2 mL)* salt
1 tbsp. *(15 mL)* sugar
3 tbsp. *(45 mL)* chilled butter
1 cup *(250 mL)* milk

In a bowl, combine all of the dry ingredients. Cut in the butter. Make a hollow in the centre of the dry ingredients. Stir in the milk slowly, stirring constantly, just until the dough is thoroughly mixed. **Caution: do not over mix**.

Drop the dough by spoonfuls on a greased cookie sheet.

An alternative is to roll out the biscuit dough on a floured board to about 1" (2.5 cm) thick and cut with a 2" (5 cm) cookie cutter – place the biscuits on a greased cookie sheet.

Bake at 450°F (230°C) for 12 to 15 minutes, or until just nicely browned on top.

Yield: approximately 12 to 13 biscuits

Variation: These Baking Powder Biscuits also make an excellent base for **Strawberry Shortcakes**. Split the cooled biscuits and spoon sweetened sliced strawberries over the bottom half. Top with sweetened whipped cream and the top half of the biscuit. Top with additional sliced berries and whipped cream.

Sliced peaches, nectarines or blueberries, etc. may be used instead of the strawberries.

Granny Olsen's hot baking powder biscuits, slathered in butter, are a complement to any meal. They can be whipped up in no time, for breakfast, lunch or supper.

Plain Muffins

It takes courage to include a recipe for Plain Muffins in these days of a hundred flavour combinations – however these are basic, easy and darn good!

2 cups *(500 mL)* flour
1 tbsp. *(15 mL)* baking powder
2 tbsp. *(30 mL)* sugar
pinch of salt
1 egg, slightly beaten
½ cup *(125 mL)* melted butter
1⅓ cups *(325 mL)* milk

Combine all of the dry ingredients in a large bowl. Make a well in the centre and pour in the liquids; stir only until thoroughly mixed.

Spoon the batter into a well-greased muffin pan, filling each cup ⅔ full.

Bake at 400°F (200°C) for 20 minutes.

Yield: 12, 2½" (6 cm) muffins

Variation: For a little variety you can make **Jam-Filled Muffins** by putting 1 small spoonful of dough in each muffin cup, top with a small spoonful of apricot or raspberry jam, then add another spoonful of dough. Sprinkle the tops with a little Cinnamon Sugar, see page 12.

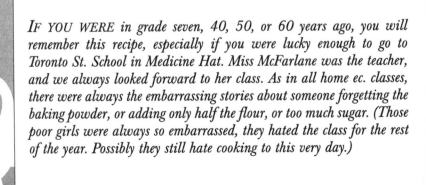

IF YOU WERE in grade seven, 40, 50, or 60 years ago, you will remember this recipe, especially if you were lucky enough to go to Toronto St. School in Medicine Hat. Miss McFarlane was the teacher, and we always looked forward to her class. As in all home ec. classes, there were always the embarrassing stories about someone forgetting the baking powder, or adding only half the flour, or too much sugar. (Those poor girls were always so embarrassed, they hated the class for the rest of the year. Possibly they still hate cooking to this very day.)

Bran Muffins

2 cups *(500 mL)* flour
½ tsp. *(2 mL)* baking soda
4 tsp. *(20 mL)* baking powder
3 cups *(750 mL)* bran (real bran)
pinch of salt
1 cup *(250 mL)* brown sugar
½ cup *(125 mL)* melted butter
2 cups *(500 mL)* buttermilk
2 eggs

Use the Muffin Method on page 10.

Put all of the dry ingredients in a large bowl. Make a well in the centre and add the liquids. Beat only enough to mix in all ingredients. Do not over beat.

Spoon the batter into greased muffin pans, filling each cup ⅔ full.

Bake at 350°F (180°C) for 25 minutes.

Yield: 18, 2¾" (7 cm) muffins

We have tried many different Bran Muffin recipes over the years – always returning to this one.

Zucchini Muffins

2 cups *(500 mL)* grated, unpeeled
   zucchini
1 cup *(250 mL)* yellow raisins
1 cup *(250 mL)* chopped pecans
3 cups *(750 mL)* flour
1 tbsp. *(15 mL)* baking powder
1 tsp. *(5 mL)* baking soda
½ tsp. *(2 mL)* salt
1 tsp. *(5 mL)* cinnamon
2 cups *(500 mL)* sugar
4 eggs
1 cup *(250 mL)* vegetable oil
1 tsp. *(5 mL)* vanilla

Wash and grate the zucchini; set aside. Wash the raisins and chop the pecans; set aside.

Put all of the dry ingredients into a large bowl. Make a well in the centre and add the eggs, oil and vanilla; mix thoroughly. Stir in zucchini, pecans and raisins.

Spoon the batter into greased muffin pans, filling each cup ⅔ full.

Bake at 350°F (180°C) for 25 minutes.

Yield: 24, 2¾" (7 cm) muffins

Ingrid Smith was an English girl who moved out to the country. She instilled a lot of culture, charmed us all, won our hearts and showed us how to make the most of an abundance of zucchini.

Granny Garratt

GRANNY WAS BORN in China, the daughter of a British Army Officer. The family had a private tutor during their time in both China and India. As a young teenager, she was sent home to England to finish her education.

In time she married the youngest son of a very good family. After a few years and a couple of children, they moved to Canada in the 1890s with a sum of money and a monthly allowance, which tells you that, in actuality, my grandfather was a remittance man. They settled in the area that became Winnipeg. There was not much commerce in the area and my grandfather decided against farming. It was not long before he deserted my Grandmother, leaving her scrambling, with two children, a little bit of money, and no means of support.

She could have packed up and gone home to England, but she didn't. She was too proud. Instead, with her meager resources, she built a Maternity Home and named it GARRATT HOUSE. It was a facility that served the farming community. The expectant father would bring his pregnant wife in a month before the due date, leave her, and pick up mother and baby a month after the due date.

Granny was doing quite well, when her husband returned, the result being two more children. When my father was four or five, my grandfather insisted that the family move to Alberta, to a homestead south of Medicine Hat. They were not there very long when he left again. Being the strong person she was, Granny continued on with the homestead. She raised her children alone and simply got on with life. Eventually, my grandfather became ill and returned home for Granny to care for him until he died.

I can't help but wonder if, given the same circumstances, I could be as forgiving as she was. In spite of a hard, troubled life, Granny Garratt lived to be 96, as did all of her children. Amazing!

An interesting side note. When I was in Winnipeg one time, the museum had a picture of GARRATT HOUSE, see page 21, and they made the claim that this home was situated on property that later became the corner of Portage and Main, the heart of downtown Winnipeg.

Yorkshire Pudding

3 large eggs
1 cup *(250 mL)* milk
½ tsp. *(2 mL)* salt
1 cup *(250 mL)* flour

shortening or roast drippings for
    the pan

Put the eggs, milk, salt and flour into the bowl of an electric mixer or a blender. Beat for at least 2 minutes. Check the consistency, it should be like medium cream.

Refrigerate the batter for 1 hour.

Preheat the oven to 450°F (230°C).

If you are using muffin tins, put a little of the drippings into each muffin cup. Put the pan into the hot oven, so the fat and pan get good and hot.

Beat the batter 1 more minute, then pour into the hot pans, up to ¾ full, and pop into the oven quickly.

Bake for 20 to 25 minutes, or until the puddings are crusty and brown. **Do not open the oven until the puddings are done.**

Yield: 12 puddings

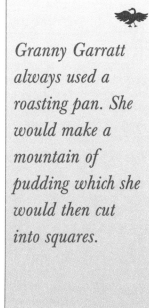

Granny Garratt always used a roasting pan. She would make a mountain of pudding which she would then cut into squares.

Garratt House, Portage and Main, Winnipeg, Manitoba, circa 1890

Dumplings

When was the last time you had stew and dumplings? Try these with beef, lamb or chicken stews.

2 cups *(500 mL)* flour
4 tsp. *(20 mL)* baking powder
½ tsp. *(2 mL)* salt
2 tsp. *(10 mL)* sugar
2 tbsp. *(30 mL)* butter
1 egg, slightly beaten
1 cup *(250 mL)* milk

First and foremost, in order to make fluffy dumplings, you must have a good pot with a tight lid. Make sure that the pot is not too full of stew or whatever you are putting the dumplings on, or when the dumplings swell you will have stew juice all over the oven.

In a large bowl, combine the dry ingredients and cut in the butter or shortening as you would for pie crust.

Add the beaten egg and milk. Stir quickly, just until all ingredients are mixed in. You may have to add a little more milk at this point, but do not dilly dally.

Carefully drop the batter by spoonfuls onto the surface of the hot (bubbling) stew, see page 97.

Put the lid on and put the stew back in the oven at 350°F (180°C) for 20 minutes. No matter how curious you are, DO NOT LIFT THE LID before the time is up.

Serves 4

Variations: For ***Herbed Dumplings***, add 1 to 2 tbsp. (15 to 30 mL) each of 2 to 3 finely minced herbs to the basic dumpling recipe to complement the flavour of your stew. Some combinations to try are: parsley and basil, parsley and green onion or chives, or parsley and thyme.

Breakfasts
&
Brunches

Pancakes

Waking up Sunday morning to the heavenly aroma of Dad's pancakes wafting from the kitchen is one of my fondest childhood memories.

2 cups *(500 mL)* flour
1 tbsp. *(15 mL)* sugar
1 tsp. *(5 mL)* baking soda
1 tbsp. *(15 mL)* baking powder
pinch of salt
4 eggs, beaten
4 tbsp. *(60 mL)* melted butter
2½ cups *(625 mL)* buttermilk

Make sure the mixing bowl is a decent size. Combine all of the dry ingredients in the bowl. Make a well in the centre; add the eggs, butter and milk. Add the milk as you beat the batter – you may need more or less milk.

The pancake batter should not be too thick, or too thin – it should be of a pouring consistency.

Putting the batter in a large jug makes pouring the batter onto the griddle much easier, and not as messy.

The griddle must be hot. Melt butter on the hot griddle, or spray with non-stick spray. Try 1 or 2 small pancakes to see if the batter or griddle need adjusting. Pour the batter onto the hot griddle. When bubbles appear on the top of the pancakes, turn them and brown the other side.

Serve hot with butter and syrup, or spread with jam, or top with sliced fruit or berries and whipped cream.

Serves 4

PANCAKES OR WAFFLES Sunday morning was a custom that we continued for my children and grandchildren as long as there was family around. At one point in our lives, when we lived in the country, my son Greg and his family lived about two miles away and came every Sunday for their favourite breakfast. Soon their family dog, Maggie, was begging to come along to help out with the leftovers. If for some reason, the family could not come, Maggie would take it upon herself to trot the two miles and appear on my doorstep by herself. She never came any other time, only on Sunday mornings. To this day, we don't know how Maggie knew it was Sunday. Was that heavenly aroma calling her from two miles away?

Waffles

2 cups *(500 mL)* flour
2 tbsp. *(30 mL)* sugar
pinch of salt
4 tsp. *(20 mL)* baking powder
4 egg yolks
½ cup *(125 mL)* melted butter
2 cups *(500 mL)* milk, more or less
4 egg whites, stiffly beaten

Combine the dry ingredients in a large bowl. Make a well in the centre and add the egg yolks, melted butter and milk.

Beat the egg whites until stiff. Gently fold the batter into egg whites until smooth. Do not beat the batter, fold it gently.

The batter must be heavier than a pancake batter but not too stiff. If you feel it is too stiff add a little more milk or water.

If your waffle iron is NOT non-stick, preheat it and brush it with vegetable oil or spray with a non-stick spray, otherwise, just preheat it.

Pour the batter to about ¼" (1 cm) of the edge of the grids. Close the lid and DO NOT OPEN it until the waffle iron has stopped steaming and the waffle is golden brown.

Serve waffles immediately or keep them warm in a 200°F (93°C) oven until all of the waffles are ready to serve. Serve with butter and syrup or fruit and whipped cream

Serves 4

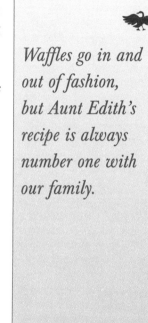

Waffles go in and out of fashion, but Aunt Edith's recipe is always number one with our family.

WHEN DAN AND KATINA *were traveling in California, they stopped at a Waffle & Pancake Specialty House. When the waitress came for their order, Dan challenged, "My mom makes the best waffles in the world. Knowing that, does the Chef recommend that I order them?" The girl headed for the kitchen. A few minutes she later came back to report, "The Chef says that you are about to have the second best waffles in the world!"*

Was that Chef a diplomat, or what?

Crêpes

This recipe can be used for both sweet and savory crêpes. The good part is that they can be made the day ahead. Put waxed paper between them, then put them in a container with a lid, to keep them from drying out, and refrigerate.

³⁄₄ cup *(175 mL)* flour
1 tsp. *(5 mL)* sugar
¹⁄₂ tsp. *(2 mL)* salt
4 eggs
2 tbsp. *(30 mL)* vegetable oil
1 cup *(250 mL)* milk

Put all of the ingredients in a large bowl. With an electric mixer, beat very well. The batter should be fairly thin.

Use a nonstick pan, maybe even spray it a little.

Pour the batter from a good pouring jug into a hot frying pan or crêpe pan. (The pan must be light enough for you to handle readily.) Pour just enough batter to barely coat the bottom of the pan, roll the pan around to get the batter to spread as far as you can.

Let the crêpe cook only until it starts to bubble. Flip or turn the crêpe over; the second side needs very little cooking time.

It may take a little practice, but I'm sure you will get the hang of it after 1 or 2 tries.

Yield: 10, 8" (20 cm) crêpes

When you are cracking eggs, crack them on the counter instead of on the edge of the bowl. That way you won't get tiny pieces of shell in the bowl.

Layered French Crêpes

10, 6" *(15 cm)* crêpes, see crêpe recipe on page 26 (Make crêpes the day ahead if you wish.)

Cheese Sauce:
½ cup *(125 mL)* butter
½ cup *(125 mL)* flour
1 tsp. *(5 mL)* salt
⅛ tsp. *(0.5 mL)* pepper
½ tsp. *(2 mL)* dry mustard
2½ cups *(625 mL)* milk
1½ cups *(375 mL)* grated cheese

Spinach-Mushroom Filling:
6 tbsp. *(90 mL)* butter
10 oz. *(283 g)* pkg. frozen chopped spinach, thawed and drained
½ lb. *(250 g)* mushrooms, chopped

Garnish:
1 large mushroom, sliced
1 tbsp. *(30 mL)* chopped parsley

Prepare the crêpes.

Sauce: Melt the butter in a saucepan, add flour, salt, pepper and dry mustard. Stir until smooth. Add the milk slowly, stirring until thick. Stir in the cheese until smooth.

Filling: Drain the spinach well. In a 10" (25 cm) pan, melt the butter and sauté the spinach and mushrooms. Remove from the heat.

Reserve ½ cup (125 mL) of the cheese sauce. Combine the rest of the sauce with the spinach mushroom mixture.

Preheat oven to 350°F (180°C).

To assemble the crêpes, use a heat-proof buttered serving dish, a 12" (30 cm) quiche pan works well. Place 1 crêpe on the dish. Spread with ½ cup (125 mL) filling. Top with another crêpe, continue stacking and filling, ending with a crêpe on top. (To keep the crêpe stack from slipping while it bakes, insert 3 metal "turkey" skewers down through the crêpes.) Cover completely with foil. Heat the layered crêpes in the oven for 20 minutes. Remove the foil (and the skewers).

Spoon the reserved cheese sauce over the crêpes. Garnish with mushroom slices and parsley. Cut into wedges to serve.

Serves 6 to 8

This is a very tasty brunch or lunch dish. It also looks spectacular.

Mushroom Crêpes

If you have a passion for the distinctive flavour of mushrooms, this is a simple yet elegant dish that is perfect for brunch or even for a light supper. It is also a simple make-ahead recipe that helps a busy cook stay organized.

1 crêpe recipe from page 26

Mushroom Filling:
½ lb. *(250 g)* mushrooms, sliced
2 tbsp. *(30 mL)* butter
2 tbsp. *(30 mL)* flour
½ tsp. *(2 mL)* salt
1 cup *(250 mL)* light cream
1 tbsp. *(15 mL)* sherry
2 tsp. *(10 mL)* lemon juice

Topping:
2 tbsp. *(30 mL)* Parmesan
½ tsp. *(2 mL)* paprika
2 tbsp. *(30 mL)* butter, melted

Make the crêpes ahead of time.

Filling: In a large frying pan, simmer the mushrooms in butter for 5 minutes. Blend the remaining filling ingredients together and pour over the mushrooms. Simmer until the sauce has thickened. Cool the filling.

Roll the filling in the crêpes and put them seam side down in a 9" (23 cm) square pan.

Sprinkle the crêpes with Parmesan and paprika. Drizzle with melted butter.

Bake at 350°F (180°C) for 30 minutes.

Yield: 10 to 12 crêpes

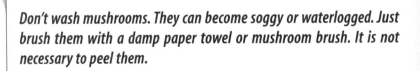

Don't wash mushrooms. They can become soggy or waterlogged. Just brush them with a damp paper towel or mushroom brush. It is not necessary to peel them.

Grand Marnier Midnight French Toast

12 eggs
½ cup *(125 mL)* **cream**
½ tsp. *(2 mL)* **vanilla**
1 orange, grated zest of
2 tbsp. *(30 mL)* **orange juice**
2 tbsp. *(30 mL)* **Grand Marnier**
1 loaf of French Bread cut in
1" *(2.5 cm)* slices

Combine the eggs, cream, vanilla, orange zest and liqueur in a large flat pan or dish. Place the bread slices in the dish in a single layer, making sure all slices are coated. Cover the dish with a lid or plastic wrap and put it in the refrigerator.

In the morning, place the bread slices on a well-greased 12 x 16" (30 x 41 cm) cookie sheet. Do not crowd.

Bake at 375°F (190°C) for 20 to 25 minutes.

Serve as is or serve with syrup, or with sliced fresh fruit or berries and whipped cream.

Serves 6

Variations: For **Maple Grand Marnier French Toast**, substitute maple syrup for the cream.

For **Pecan Grand Marnier French Toast**, warm 1 cup (250 mL) of chopped pecans in ¼ cup (60 mL) melted butter and stir in ½ cup (125 mL) brown sugar. Drizzle over the bread slices just before baking. You may also add ¼ tsp. (1 mL) of cinnamon to the egg mixture.

The flavours in this brunch dish are a luxurious combination of Grand Marnier, vanilla and cream. It's hard to believe it's also a convenience dish. Your family or guests will love you for this one.

Spanish Omelette

This is the recipe to use when unexpected company walks through the door just before mealtime. It's perfect for brunch, lunch or supper. Quick and easy, it will save the day for you. It also looks very impressive!

1 large onion, chopped
4 tbsp. *(60 mL)* olive oil
2 large potatoes, cooked
  and diced
1 cup *(250 mL)* sliced fresh or
  canned mushrooms
1 cup *(250 mL)* green vegetables,
  peas, beans OR asparagus
¾ cup *(175 mL)* cubed ham
1 tomato, cubed
1 cup *(250 mL)* grated yellow cheese
1 tomato, sliced, for garnish
asparagus spears for garnish
6 eggs, slightly beaten

In an 11 or 12" (28 or 30 cm) cast iron frying pan (or any ovenproof frying pan) sauté the onions in the olive oil.

Add the vegetables, except for the cubed tomatoes, 1 at a time and allow them to heat through. Add the ham and cubed tomatoes and heat through.

Sprinkle the cheese over the tomatoes; arrange the sliced tomatoes and asparagus spears on top. Pour the beaten eggs evenly over the entire surface.

Bake at 350°F (180°C) for 30 minutes.

Serves 6

Pictured on page 33.

MY SISTER-IN-LAW Viv Edwards acquired this recipe when she lived in Spain. She tells me that there are as many recipes for Spanish omelette as there are women in Spain. The Spanish like it hot or cold, in fact, it is a favourite for picnics and is often served at room temperature in tapas bars, cut into bite-sized squares.

Quiche Lorraine

pastry for a double-crust pie, see
page 130

1 cup *(250 mL)* sliced onions
1 tbsp. *(15 mL)* butter
4 slices bacon, fried crisp and
crumbled
1½ cups *(375 mL)* grated Swiss OR
Cheddar cheese
4 eggs beaten
pinch EACH of salt, pepper
and nutmeg
1 cup *(250 mL)* cream
1 cup *(250 mL)* milk

Prepare the crust and carefully line a 12" (30 cm) quiche dish.

Sauté the onions in butter. Sprinkle the sautéed onions evenly over the crust. Sprinkle the crumbled bacon and the grated cheese over the onions. (Prepare to this stage, if you are making an hour or 2 ahead, and refrigerate.)

Beat together the eggs and seasonings; combine with the cream and milk. Pour carefully over the ingredients in the pie shell.

Bake the quiche on the lower rack of the oven at 450°F (230°C) for 10 minutes, then turn down the heat to 350°F (180°C) for 25 to 30 minutes.

(Add an extra 10 minutes to baking time if the quiche has been refrigerated.)

Serves 6

Variations: Swiss cheeses, Gruyère or Emmenthal, are traditional but many variations are possible. Try half Cheddar and half Swiss cheese. Cubed ham or flaked crab may be substituted for the bacon. Add chopped chives for flavour and presentation.

This adaptation of the classic recipe works well on those occasions when you are not exactly sure when the company is coming. You can have it ready ahead of time and pop it into the oven 40 minutes before you want to serve it. Serve with salad and homemade buns.

Cheese Soufflé

Everyone seems to like Cheese Soufflé. It seems to amaze people that it rises so well, but there is no secret, just follow instructions and Voila ! When I canvassed my family about their favourite recipes to go into this cookbook, Cheese Soufflé was on every list.

½ cup *(125 mL)* butter
½ cup *(125 mL)*flour
½ tsp. *(2 mL)* salt
2 cups *(500 mL)* milk

½ lb. *(225 g)* grated Cheddar cheese
8 egg yolks, slightly beaten
8 egg whites, stiffly beaten

In a medium saucepan, make a **white sauce (béchamel)**, by melting the butter, and stirring in the flour and salt. Stir in the cheese, mixing thoroughly. Add yolks and beat until smooth.

Beat the egg whites until stiff. Fold the whites into the cheese sauce.

Pour the soufflé mixture into a 9 x 4" (23 x 10 cm) straight-sided soufflé dish. **Do not butter the dish as the soufflé must climb the sides.**

Bake at 475°F (250°C) for 10 minutes, then lower the heat to 400°F (200°C) for 25 minutes. **DO NOT OPEN THE OVEN DOOR.** The soufflé drops a little when you take it out of the oven. It drops a lot more when you cut into it.

Serves 6 to 8

Note: If your soufflé dish is less than 7" (10 cm) across and under 4" (18 cm) high, put an aluminum foil sleeve or collar on it. To make the sleeve, select a piece of foil about 2" (5 cm) longer than the circumference of your dish. Fold the foil in quarters, lengthwise. Wrap the foil around the outside of the baking dish, with the foil extending about 2" (5 cm) above the rim of the dish, and tie it in place with cotton or sisal kitchen string (not plastic string).

Variations: This recipe can be adapted to use up all the leftover bits and pieces of cheese in your refrigerator. I've had some serendipitous combinations, both interesting and tasty. Also, add a pinch or 2 of ground nutmeg for variety.

BREAKFAST & BRUNCH

Spanish Omelette, page 30

Appetizers & Drinks

Pepper & Cheese Roll

Doug Cairns was the most unlikely person you could ever find to have a recipe to share. However, his creamy cheese roll is delicious. Use aged or mild Cheddar to suit your taste.

1 lb. *(500 g)* cream cheese
1 lb. *(500 g)* Cheddar cheese, grated
13 oz. *(375 mL)* jar sweet banana peppers, drained, seeded
½ cup *(125 mL)* chopped nuts OR sesame seeds*

Put the room temperature cream cheese into a food processor; add the grated Cheddar cheese and process until smooth. Add the banana peppers in chunks and pulse the processor until the peppers are incorporated but are still in pieces, not pulverized.

Remove the cheese mixture from the processor and chill for at least an hour, until firm enough to shape. Form balls or rolls.

Roll the balls in chopped nuts or roasted sesame seeds. Refrigerate.

Serve with your favourite crackers.

Yield: 2, 4" (10 cm) balls or 2 rolls, 2 x 8" (5 x 20 cm)

* The nuts and seeds have more flavour if they are roasted.

IN 1935, JAPAN invited a Junior Canadian Team to go to Japan and compete with their fledgling hockey team. A Saskatchewan team, The Battleford Millers, were chosen to go. Doug Cairns was the captain of the team. Happily, the Millers won. Later, in the 1940s, Doug was a favourite player for the Calgary Stampeders. Nicknamed "Crafty" Cairns, he was, again, captain. They won the Allen cup in 1946 and made Alberta, and especially Calgary, very proud.

In 1972, we moved next door to the Cairns in Springbank. They were wonderful neighbours. Life was usually peaceful and quiet, but at least once a summer, on a lovely, sunny day, I would come home from town to find Mr. C. with some of his old hockey buddies sitting in the lounge chairs by our swimming pool, drinking our beer. To complete the scene, his black lab, Lady, would be showing how clever she was by fetching sticks from our pool.

We had a list of "Pool Rules" and "NO DOGS IN THE POOL" was pretty high on that list! My shouting and hollering only frightened Lady, who would immediately jump out of the pool, run over to my glass sliding doors and shake all the water off that black shiny coat of hers. The more screeching I did the more Lady shook, and the more the group laughed, it made their day!! (Maybe it made mine too.)

Devilled Eggs

6 hard-boiled eggs
2 scant tsp. *(10 mL)* lemon juice
2½ tbsp. *(37 mL)* mayonnaise
¼ tsp. *(1 mL)* dry mustard powder
salt and pepper to taste
sprinkle of paprika

Current Options:
Tabasco
onion salt
capers
chopped dillweed
chopped chives

Peel the hard-boiled eggs and slice them in half lengthwise. Remove the yolks and place them in a small bowl.

Set the whites aside on a serving plate.

Mash the yolks with a fork, and add the remaining ingredients, except paprika. See the option list for possible additions. Continue mashing until smooth. (If you are doing larger amounts, you might want to use a food processor.)

Spoon or pipe the seasoned yolks into the whites. Sprinkle with paprika.

Yield: 12 eggs

Pictured on page 51.

An old favourite, Granny Olsen's basic recipe is truly the best. Is it possible to have a picnic or special family dinner without Devilled Eggs? Add Tabasco, capers or even a sprinkle of chopped dill or chives to suit your taste.

GRANNY OLSEN *was a city girl from Copenhagen. At the age of 18, in 1902, she married my grandpa, who had been a silver medal athlete and a world-traveled sailor. They homesteaded for a few years in South Dakota, but the lure of free land brought them to southern Saskatchewan. They had everything to learn about farming – and they did. (Today you would say they were fast learners.) When their children started arriving, Grandpa insisted that they must speak only English at home. Granny's English was always better than Grandpa's but, when I was a child, she tried to convey messages to him in Danish that were not for little ears. Grandpa always answered in English, giving away the secret. I could sense that the Danish words that followed were a little sharp.*

They became very successful farmers, due not only to that Danish determination, but also to their ability to work very hard, and always look ahead with a positive attitude – through two world wars, the depression, sandstorms and drought. (Grandpa had such a positive attitude that he was never wrong about anything as long as he lived.) We loved him anyway!

Shrimp Cocktail

My dad's specialty, his Shrimp Cocktail recipe doesn't use bottled chili sauce, but due to our prairie location he did use canned shrimp. This is one of those timeless, easy-to-prepare dishes using pantry staples.

4 cups *(1 L)* canned tomatoes
2 cups *(500 mL)* cooked fresh shrimp
  OR 2, 7 oz. *(400 g)* cans of shrimp
½ cup *(125 mL)* French dressing
1 tbsp. *(15 mL)* horseradish
1 tsp. *(5 mL)* Worcestershire sauce
salt and pepper to taste

shredded lettuce
½ cup *(125 mL)* mayonnaise OR
  sour cream
dash paprika

Strain the tomatoes and press them through a sieve.

In a bowl, mix the tomato purée with the shrimp, French dressing, horseradish, Worcestershire, salt and pepper and chill until serving time.

Serve the shrimp in cocktail glasses with a little shredded lettuce in the bottom of each glass.

A dab of mayonnaise or sour cream, and a sprinkle of paprika, gives it a nice finishing touch.

Serves 8

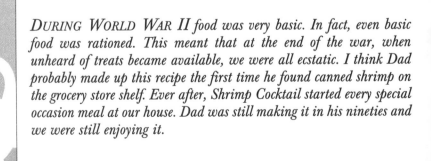

DURING WORLD WAR II food was very basic. In fact, even basic food was rationed. This meant that at the end of the war, when unheard of treats became available, we were all ecstatic. I think Dad probably made up this recipe the first time he found canned shrimp on the grocery store shelf. Ever after, Shrimp Cocktail started every special occasion meal at our house. Dad was still making it in his nineties and we were still enjoying it.

Shrimp Dip

8 oz. *(250 g)* pkg. cream cheese
¾ cup *(175 mL)* mayonnaise
l tbsp. *(15 mL)* ketchup
1 tsp. *(5 mL)* Tabasco
½ cup *(125 mL)* finely chopped celery
¾ cup *(175 mL)* finely chopped onion
7 oz. *(200 g)* can broken shrimp

Put all of the ingredients into a medium bowl and beat with an electric mixer until smooth.

Chill the dip for several hours to allow the flavours to blend.

Serve with chips or taco chips or an assortment of your favourite crackers.

Serves 6

Pictured on page 51.

This is our all-time, number one family favourite dip recipe. It came from Hazel McKee.

HAZEL WAS A good friend and a real character, as well as a delightful story teller. I have to admit that she told my "kid" stories better than I did. When I listened to her rendition of some of their childhood escapades I hardly recognized them. To say that she could "gild the lily" was a huge understatement.

When Danny was four, Hazel had us over for Sunday supper. The table was dazzling with silver, crystal, candles, the works. Instead of having Dan sit next to me, where I could control his actions a little, she placed him next to her. Big Mistake! The first thing he did was put his elbow on the table. With head on hand, he grabbed the white napkin with his other hand and shouted, "Hey Mom, it's not a sandwich, you can't eat it." Then he proceeded to grab both of his forks and let the world know, "Hey, I have two forks – look – two forks, Mom, I don't need two forks." It got worse.

He was out of my reach and not listening to one word from me.

That very evening, when we got home, there was a little refresher on table manners. From that day on Sunday dinner became manners night, we practised and discussed the many aspects and pitfalls of good and bad table manners. The boys have all thanked me on many occasions for the lessons, but I feel the real thanks should go to Hazel, for putting Danny out of my reach, and making me aware that there was a real need for a little instruction.

Salmon Mousse

My niece Lindy Lakusta contributed this smooth flavourful mousse. Lemon juice, white wine, Tabasco and Worcestershire add zest to the creamy salmon mixture.

1 tbsp. *(7 g)* (1 env.) **unflavoured gelatin**

¼ cup *(60 mL)* **cold dry white wine**

½ cup *(125 mL)* **boiling water**

⅓ cup *(75 mL)* **mayonnaise**

⅓ cup *(75 mL)* **sour cream**

1 tbsp. *(15 mL)* **fresh lemon juice**

1 tbsp. *(15 mL)* **minced onion**

1 tsp. *(5 mL)* **salt**

¼ tsp. *(1 mL)* **paprika**

⅛ tsp. *(0.5 mL)* **Tabasco**

½ tsp. *(2 mL)* **Worcestershire sauce**

2 cups *(500 mL)* **flaked, cooked red salmon**

1 cup *(250 mL)* **whipping cream**

In a large heatproof bowl, soften the gelatin in the cold wine. Slowly add boiling water and stir until gelatin dissolves. Let cool at room temperature.

Whisk in the mayonnaise, sour cream, lemon juice, onion, salt, paprika, Tabasco and Worcestershire until well blended. Refrigerate until the mixture begins to thicken, about 20 minutes.

Beat in the salmon until smooth.

In another large bowl, whip the cream until soft peaks form.

Fold the whipped cream into the salmon mixture, one-third at a time, until well blended.

Pour the mousse into an oiled 6-cup (1.5 L) mould. Cover and refrigerate until firm (overnight).

Unmould on a serving plate. Serve chilled with assorted crackers.

Serves 8

MY SISTER-IN-LAW Kay had six boys and one girl, Lindy. I had three boys. Now you might think that having one girl, in the midst of nine boys, we would have spoilt her terribly – not so. The only times I can remember her getting preferential treatment was on the weekends when we all got together at their home or ours. By four in the afternoon, having been in and out all day, with bathroom trips and drinks of water, the dads would take the boys out to play football, or baseball or hockey, depending on the season. Kay and Lindy and I would quickly lock the door, put our feet up and drink coffee for half an hour. (The game plan was that the players and coaches would have to be bleeding to get in before the time was up.) Lindy loved that special time as much as we did. We doted on her but we did not spoil her!

When Lindy tells this story she claims that at times she had to go play football too. That may have happened, but only if she was whining a lot that day!

Texas Cheese Wafers

1 cup *(250 mL)* butter
2 cups *(500 mL)* flour
8 oz. *(250 g)* grated sharp cheese
½ tsp. *(2 mL)* cayenne pepper
½ tsp. *(2 mL)* salt
¼ cup *(60 mL)* roasted sesame seeds
2 cups *(500 mL)* Rice Krispies

Cream together the butter, flour and cheese. Add the cayenne, salt, sesame seeds and Rice Krispies. Mix well.

Drop the dough by spoonfuls onto greased cookie sheets. Flatten with the bottom of a glass. Dip the glass into water from time to time to keep it from sticking.

Bake the wafers at 350°F (180°C) for 25 minutes. Watch carefully as they burn very easily.

Yield: 36 to 40 wafers

Pictured on page 51.

Rich and zippy! These little wafers are perfect with a glass of wine, but be careful, they are addictive.

Appetizer Math

How many appetizers do you need per person for a party?

4 to 5 per guest before an early meal
6 to 7 per guest before a late meal
8 to 9 per guest if no meal is served

Now, remember that common sense rules here. If you have larger appetizers, of course you will not need as many as when you have small finger-food portions. Most of the appetizers in this book are larger than hors d'oeuvres. I feel that the above numbers are nothing more than a good guess, arrived at after over 50 years of cooking for family and friends.

Pork, Veal & Chicken Liver Terrine

A terrine is a pâte baked in a bacon or pork-fat-lined dish called a terrine. Jake Lawson's version is very tasty, looks wonderful, and has the added bonus that it is a wonderful make ahead appetizer.

1 lb. *(500 g)* sliced bacon
2 tbsp. *(30 mL)* butter
1 medium onion, chopped
1 garlic clove, finely chopped
1 lb. *(500 g)* ground pork
1 lb. *(500 g)* ground veal
½ lb. *(250 g)* chicken livers, finely chopped
pinch EACH allspice, cloves, nutmeg, cinnamon, thyme, sage, any or all
2 eggs, slightly beaten
¾ cup *(175 mL)* heavy cream
3 tbsp. *(45 mL)* brandy
salt and pepper to taste
6 slices of cooked ham

Line a 2-quart (2 L) loaf pan with the bacon, leaving a few strips for the top.

Melt the butter in a frying pan and sauté the onion and garlic.

In a large bowl, combine all of the ingredients, except the sliced ham and bacon. Mix thoroughly.

Press half of the meat mixture into the loaf pan over the bacon.

Next, lay the ham neatly on top, then press the remaining meat mixture over the ham. Top with the remaining strips of bacon. Cover with foil.

Set the terrine into a pan of boiling water – the water should reach halfway up the terrine. Bake at 350°F (180°C) for 1½ hours, or until a meat thermometer reads 170°F (77°C). Remove from the oven and water bath. Pour off any liquid or fat.

Distribute 2 lbs. (1 kg) of weight (a couple of old flat irons or 2, 16 oz. [500 g] cans would do) on top of the foil on the terrine – to compress the meat. Let cool. Refrigerate for a day. Remove the weights. Turn the terrine out on a platter and slice thinly. Serve with a French loaf.

Serves 12

JAKE IS A VERY successful "A" type person. Everything he does, he does well. (Just in passing, if you are going to do anything at all for him, make sure you do it right, or you will hear about it!)

Picture this – Jake always took pride in the cars he drove. He traded them in often, and always kept them scrupulously clean, inside and out. One year he got a new Jaguar, a lovely dark blue. He was very pleased.

Coin-operated car washes were opening up about that time. One day there was a little dust on the car, so fastidious Jake decided to give the coin-operated wash a try. He drove into the stall with confidence, got out eagerly, and put the necessary coins into the slot, only to have the wand (which he had not picked up) spring into action like a wild, drunken, vicious snake. Six divots on the car hood later, Jake finally found the "off" button. Wanna bet the air was blue too??

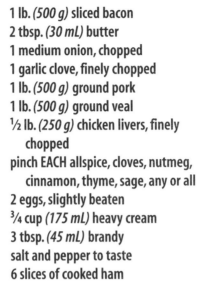

Bruschetta

2 lbs. *(1 kg)* Roma tomatoes, chopped
2 garlic cloves, crushed
½ cup *(125 mL)* olive oil
1 tbsp. *(15 mL)* chopped basil
salt and pepper to taste
Parmesan to sprinkle

1 French loaf

Chop the tomatoes. Add crushed garlic, olive oil, basil, salt and pepper. Refrigerate for a couple of hours to allow the flavours of the garlic, basil, olive oil and tomatoes to blend.

Fire up the barbecue or turn the oven to broil.

Cut the bread in 1" (2.5 cm) slices. Spoon some of the tomato mixture onto the bread; sprinkle with Parmesan and, if broiling, place on a cookie sheet. Place under the broiler.

If barbecuing, place the Bruschetta directly on the grill, in an area that is not too hot. In either case, watch verrrrry carefully.

Serves 6 to 8

Pictured on page 105.

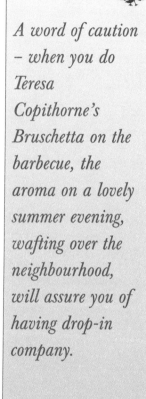

A word of caution – when you do Teresa Copithorne's Bruschetta on the barbecue, the aroma on a lovely summer evening, wafting over the neighbourhood, will assure you of having drop-in company.

EVERYBODY LOVES TERESA. *You never doubt what is on her mind, she "tells it like it is." By the way, she is Italian by birth, Canadian by choice. You may be wondering what her nationality has to do with Bruschetta? Well, simply put, Teresa puts 2 or 3 times more garlic in anything she makes than we Canadians ever dream of. Soooo, if you have the nerve, go for it, 4 to 6 cloves of garlic. It's delicious.*

Spanakopita

A Greek treat! Eleanor Mentis is my daughter-in-law Katina's aunt. The Mentis (Mentzelopoulos) family came to this country from Greece several years after the war. They brought old country charm and exceptional recipes that I have been lucky enough to have them share with me.

½ lb. *(250 g)* feta cheese
¼ lb. *(125 g)* Asiago OR Gruyère cheese
¼ lb. *(125 g)* farmer's OR cream cheese
½ cup *(125 mL)* chopped, thawed, frozen spinach
1 tbsp. *(15 mL)* raw millet (optional)
1 egg
1 tsp. *(5 mL)* parsley
¼ tsp. *(1 mL)* dillweed
pepper to taste

1 lb. *(454 g)* pkg. phyllo dough
¼ lb. *(125 g)* butter, melted

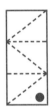

Crumble or shred the various cheeses into a large bowl. Drain and chop the spinach. Add the spinach and remaining ingredients, except the phyllo and butter, to the cheeses; mix thoroughly. You are now ready to wrap.

The phyllo dough should be at room temperature. It must be handled very carefully as it is delicate. Have a clean damp tea towel handy. Open the package and leave the waxed paper on top. Cover the waxed paper with the damp cloth. Remove 1 sheet of phyllo at a time. Place it on a plastic cutting board and brush it with melted butter.

The phyllo sheets are 12 x 16" (30 x 41 cm), cut them in half to make 12 x 8" (30 x 20 cm) sheets. Brushing each surface with butter, fold the 12" (30 cm) in half to make 6 x 8" (15 x 20 cm) rectangles, then in half again to make 3 x 8" (8 x 20 cm) rectangles, you now have 4 layers.

Put 1 spoonful of filling in the bottom corner of the phyllo and fold it in a triangular shape from bottom to top. Place the filled triangles on cookie sheets. Work fairly quickly as you don't want the triangles to dry out before you bake them.

Bake at 325°F (160°C) for 45 minutes.

Yield: about 34 to 36 Spanakopita

Pictured on page 51.

When I make these – I make enough to put them in the deep freeze. They freeze very well. Pack the unbaked Spanakopita in a good plastic container with a lid, with waxed paper between the layers. From the deep freeze, put them on a cookie sheet and into a 400°F (200°C) oven for 20 minutes.

Stuffed Mushroom Caps

16, 1½-2" *(4-5 cm)* wide
  mushrooms

2 tbsp. *(30 mL)* butter
2 tbsp. *(30 mL)* minced onions
½ cup *(125 mL)* cottage cheese
¾ tsp. *(3 mL)* Worcestershire sauce
few drops Tabasco
salt and pepper to taste
½ cup *(125 mL)* Parmesan cheese

Clean the mushrooms. Remove and chop the stems.

In a frying pan, melt the butter and add the minced onions and chopped mushroom stems. Simmer until the onions are translucent. Add the cottage cheese, Worcestershire sauce, Tabasco, salt and pepper.

Spoon the filling into the mushroom caps and place them in an ovenproof pan that suits the size. Sprinkle with Parmesan.

Bake at 400°F (200°C) for 15 to 20 minutes. Watch these verrrrrrrry carefully.

Serves 8

Variations: For **Spicy Sausage-Stuffed Mushrooms**, clean the mushrooms as above. Sauté ½ lb. (250 g) spicy Italian or Greek or Cajun sausage and 1 large minced garlic clove. Crumble the cooked sausage and add the chopped mushroom stems and onions; sauté as above. Stir in ¼ cup (60 mL) of fresh breadcrumbs and 2 tbsp. (30 mL) chopped parsley. Spoon the sausage filling into the mushroom caps. Sprinkle with Parmesan or more bread crumbs and bake as above.

Stuffed Mushroom Caps work well as either an appetizer or a side dish.

Chili Cheese Squares

If you are feeling rushed, and find you have to make appetizers for a lot of people, or have to take something to a potluck – Chili Cheese Squares are not only quick and easy, but you probably have all the ingredients in your kitchen.

10 eggs
dash Tabasco
dash Worcestershire
½ cup *(125 mL)* flour
1 tsp. *(5 mL)* baking powder
1 scant tsp. *(5 mL)* salt
¾ cup *(175 mL)* melted butter
1 lb. *(500 g)* Havarti, shredded
2 cups *(500 mL)* cottage cheese
6 oz. *(170 mL)* jar red chilies, diced

Preheat the oven to 400°F (200°C). Butter an 11 x 16" (28 x 41 cm) baking pan with edges.

In a large bowl, beat the eggs. Add the Tabasco and Worcestershire. Stir in the dry ingredients, then add the melted butter and cheeses. Blend well and fold in the chilies.

Spread the batter evenly over the baking pan. Bake for 40 to 45 minutes.

Cut into 40 pieces and serve warm. This appetizer can be frozen and reheated just before serving.

Yield: 40 squares

Vinegar is a wonderful product. Use a cupful once in a while in your dishwasher. It takes away the scale and buildup. A cupful in your humidifier once a month, makes cleaning it easier. Also, put a little in the water you are using to clean your tile or linoleum. If you want your hair to shine like it did when you were young – use a little vinegar in the rinse water.

Triple Threat Party Punch

2 cups *(500 mL)* frozen mixed sliced
  fruit and/or berries
26 oz. *(750 mL)* vodka
26 oz. *(750 mL)* rye
26 oz. *(750 mL)* cherry wine
26 oz. *(750 mL)* cranberry cocktail
12½ oz. *(355 g)* frozen orange juice
  concentrate
4 qts. *(4 L)* pink cream soda
1 orange, thinly sliced
1 lemon, thinly sliced
ice cubes

All ingredients should be chilled ahead of time and the fruit or berries need to be kept frozen.

When making the punch, put the frozen fruit into the punch bowl.

Pour the chilled liquor, wine and juices over the frozen fruit.

Add the cream soda, lemon and orange slices as the guests come in the door.

Serves 30

Pictured on page 51.

Note: In this day and age, when we are all conscious of the dangers of alcohol and driving, it is a good idea to do the math. Four ounces (115 mL) of liquor per adult is more than ample – adjust your recipe to the size of the party.

Get out the punch bowl. This punch looks lovely.

Puerto Vallarta Margarita

sea salt*
lime wedge

3 ice cubes
1½ oz. *(45 mL)* tequila
½ oz. *(15 mL)* Cointreau OR
  Triple Sec
½ oz. *(15 mL)* fresh lime juice

Place the sea salt in a saucer. Rub the rim of a glass with the lime wedge and turn the top of the glass in the salt to coat the rim. Place the ice cubes in the glass.

Combine the tequila, Cointreau and lime juice and pour over the ice cubes in the glass.

Serves 1

Pictured on page 87.

To enjoy the essence of a Margarita – shut your eyes, taste the salt, sip the tequila, and you can feel the ocean breeze and the warm sun on your face.

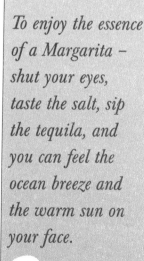

* The salt on the rim of the glass is not mandatory, but for many it's the best part of a Margarita.

Variation: Some Margarita versions use 2 oz. (60 mL) tequila to ½ oz. (15 mL) Cointreau to 1½ oz. (45 mL) of lime juice.

Rhubarb Cooler

This recipe of Granny Olsen's is a very old pioneer recipe. Before the days of bottled or canned soft drinks, it was served as a refreshing nonalcoholic drink. We are fortunate now to have ice – when this recipe was developed it was made and put down in the basement, down the well or, possibly, in the root cellar to cool.

6 cups *(1.5 L)* red rhubarb, finely chopped
8 cups *(2 L)* boiling water
2 cups *(500 mL)* sugar
1 cup *(250 mL)* water
4 tbsp. *(60 mL)* orange juice
4 tbsp. *(60 mL)* lemon juice

ice, when you are ready to serve

Cut up the rhubarb and place it in a large glass or stainless steel container. Pour the boiling water over the rhubarb. Cover and let steep for a few hours. Strain, saving the juice and throwing away the pulp.

While the rhubarb steeps, make a sugar syrup by placing the sugar and water in a saucepan and simmering until the sugar is dissolved. Cool.

Combine the rhubarb juice, lemon and orange juices and, finally, the sugar syrup. Chill. Serve over ice cubes.

Serves 8 to 10

THERE IS AN EXPRESSION, "When winter comes – then spring is sure to follow." Sure evidence of spring was the green curly shoots, followed by the rich red stalks of rhubarb poking through the warm rich earth. It was newsworthy enough to pass along to a neighbour. "My rhubarb is up," brought with it the eager anticipation of everything else the ground would yield in the coming seasons.

The garden was my Olsen grandparents' form of relaxation, to be enjoyed in the evening when all the day's real work was done.

Party-Time Eggnog

6 egg yolks, beaten
¾ cup *(175 mL)* berry or fruit sugar
   (superfine)
pinch of salt
2½ cups *(625 mL)* light cream
2 cups *(500 mL)* milk
1 cup *(250 mL)* white rum
½ cup *(125 mL)* brandy
2 cups *(500 mL)* whipping cream
6 egg whites
pinch of nutmeg

Put the beaten egg yolks into the top of a double boiler over simmering water. Add the sugar and salt slowly and continue to beat. Add the light cream and milk and continue stirring until you feel it has heated enough so that the eggs are cooked, until the mixture coats a metal spoon.

Set the yolk mixture aside to cool. Once it is cool, mix in the liquor.

Beat the whipping cream until stiff.

In a separate bowl, beat the egg whites until stiff.

Gently fold the whipped cream and the egg whites into the yolk mixture, being careful to not break down the volume of cream and whites. Pour into a punch bowl and sprinkle with nutmeg.

Chill and serve.

Serves 8 to 10

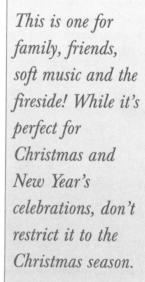

This is one for family, friends, soft music and the fireside! While it's perfect for Christmas and New Year's celebrations, don't restrict it to the Christmas season.

When you are beating egg whites – as for Angel Food Cake, Pavlova, Soufflés – make sure you have absolutely no egg yolk in with the whites. The tiniest speck of yolk will render the egg whites unbeatable. Also, make sure that the bowl and beaters are well washed; grease-free is essential. Have the egg whites at room temperature for the maximum volume.

Granny's Eggnog

In Granny's Olsen's opinion, anyone recovering from any illness – measles, mumps, flu, cold – you name it, must, as part of the recovery program, have an eggnog daily. Otherwise you would take too long to recuperate. It sure seemed to help. I don't know if it was the plain basic ingredients, or whether it was the labour of love that nourished body and soul.

1 fresh egg
1 tbsp. *(15 mL)* sugar, brown or white
1 tsp. *(5 mL)* vanilla
1 cup *(250 mL)* milk
a good dollop of fresh cream, (real thick farm cream that is!)

Granny would beat the egg with her old wire egg beater until it was thick, then slowly add the sugar, vanilla and milk, adding the cream last of all.

We have it pretty easy now – put all of the ingredients in a blender and blend until the eggnog is the consistency of a milkshake.

Serves 1

THE PIONEER WOMEN were responsible for the health of their family members. They were the doctors, nurses, caregivers and decision makers when it came to illness within their homes. A comprehensive medical book was just about as valuable as the family bible. Household recipes for remedies were passed on from generation to generation. Among these, various poultices for colds and pneumonia were common. At that time pneumonia was a killer, something to guard against and fight at all costs. Mustard plaster was a common thing for a chest cold. I can remember having a cold when I was very young. I had my chest rubbed with goose fat and turpentine, the next step would have been the mustard plaster. I got better fast. (I felt that the cure was far worse than the ailment!)

Our Grandmothers showed a lot of wisdom regarding illness. If you were sick, or had a bad cold, you were put to bed and more or less isolated from the family, except for the caregiver. I wish the same system was in existence today. Too often sick people want to show how brave they are. Endangering themselves and others, they go to work when they really should be home in bed.

Serbian Tea

4 tsp. *(20 mL)* sugar
2 cups *(500 mL)* boiling water
1 cup *(250 mL)* plum OR pear brandy

Browning the sugar takes patience. Put it in a heavy saucepan over medium heat and stir it until it starts turning brown.

Remove the caramelized sugar from the heat and add the boiling water. Mix well. Stir until any lumps of caramelized sugar have dissolved.

Add the brandy and just barely bring to a boil. Serve hot.

Serves 3 to 4

Note: The plum or pear brandy is from Yugoslavia.

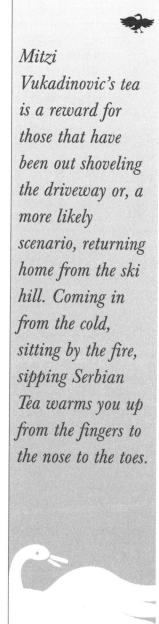

Mitzi Vukadinovic's tea is a reward for those that have been out shoveling the driveway or, a more likely scenario, returning home from the ski hill. Coming in from the cold, sitting by the fire, sipping Serbian Tea warms you up from the fingers to the nose to the toes.

MITZI AND RODDY *came to this country from Yugoslavia after the Second World War. Adapting to our culture was not always easy, but they managed through the ups and downs. They have many entertaining stories of the various misunderstandings that take place while learning a new language, in a new country.*

They were such good gardeners that every blade of grass was always facing the same way. Dandelions did not dare poke their yellow heads through that green velvet lawn. Flowers bloomed profusely and the vegetable garden was second to none. We loved Mitzi and Roddy dearly, but we were happy that we lived down the street from them and did not have to try to keep our yard looking as good as theirs. Their neighbours didn't have a chance!

Spanish Coffee

This combination of spices, orange-flavoured liqueur, brandy and coffee is world-famous – deservedly so!

lemon wedge
sugar for the rim of the glass

1 orange, grated rind of
6 tsp. *(30 mL)* sugar
½ tsp. *(2 mL)* cinnamon
½ tsp. *(2 mL)* cloves
3 tbsp. *(45 mL)* Curaçao
6 tbsp. *(90 mL)* brandy
6, ¾ cups *(175 mL)* fresh hot coffee
whipped cream for topping

Prepare 6 Spanish Coffee glasses by running a lemon wedge around the rims and then dipping the rims in a saucer filled with sugar.

In a saucepan, put the grated orange rind, sugar, cinnamon, cloves, Curaçao, and brandy. Heat almost to a boil, but not quite.

Divide the liquor mixture among the 6 glasses. Fill the glasses with fresh coffee and top each with a spoonful of whipped cream.

Serves 6

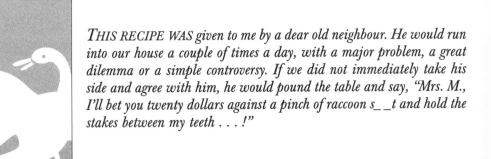

THIS RECIPE WAS given to me by a dear old neighbour. He would run into our house a couple of times a day, with a major problem, a great dilemma or a simple controversy. If we did not immediately take his side and agree with him, he would pound the table and say, "Mrs. M., I'll bet you twenty dollars against a pinch of raccoon s_ _t and hold the stakes between my teeth . . . !"

Soups

Cream of Tomato Soup

You can use this same basic recipe for any kind of cream soup, cream of asparagus, cream of squash, cream of potato, cream of mushroom, cream of corn, etc. You may want to put your vegetable of choice in the blender to make it smooth. For a little variety, you could use 1 cup (250 mL) of chicken broth instead of 1 of the cups of milk. The possibilities are endless.

2 tbsp. *(30 mL)* butter, melted
2 tbsp. *(30 mL)* flour
salt and pepper to taste
2 cups *(500 mL)* milk, warm
¼ tsp. *(1 mL)* baking soda
4 cups *(1 L)* chopped canned
    tomatoes

First you make a **roux** – in a heavy saucepan, melt the butter; when it bubbles stir in the flour, salt and pepper. That was easy! Now you create a **white sauce (béchamel)** by slowly adding the milk and stirring constantly until the sauce is thick and smooth.

Pay attention to the next item, **soda**. Add the soda BEFORE you add the tomatoes. The reason???? If you do not add the soda first, the tomatoes will make the white sauce curdle.

Stir in the tomatoes. Add more tomatoes or fewer tomatoes, or more milk or less milk, to get the right consistency and flavour for you.

Serves 4

Note: For a ***Thin White Sauce***, use 1 cup (250 mL) of milk to 1 tbsp. (15 mL) each of butter and flour.

For a ***Medium White Sauce***, use 2 tbsp. (30 mL) each of butter and flour.

For a ***Thick White Sauce***, use 3 tbsp. (45 mL) each of butter and flour.

For a ***Louisiana Roux***, cook 2 cups (500 mL) of butter, stirring constantly until it is light brown. Stir in 2 cups (500 mL) of the flour, 2 tsp. (10 mL) salt and 1 tsp. (5 mL) pepper and cook until it is a rich brown. Let the roux cool and store it in the refrigerator in a covered container.

This roux thickens and adds wonderful rich flavour to soups, stews or gravies. It is also a great timesaver as you can make it ahead and keep it on hand.

Red Pepper Soup with Sambuca

4 tbsp. *(60 mL)* butter
3 large onions
2 garlic cloves, minced
4 red peppers, roasted and
   skinned*
4, 10 oz. *(284 mL)* cans chicken broth
½ cup *(125 mL)* cream
1 tsp. *(5 mL)* salt
½ tsp. *(2 mL)* cayenne pepper
salt and pepper to taste
sambuca to taste

Melt the butter in a heavy saucepan over medium heat. Add the onions and garlic and sauté until tender. Add the roasted peppers and broth. Purée the soup in a blender in batches and return it to the pot.

Bring the soup to a boil. Stir in the cream, seasonings and sambuca. Just barely heat through.

Serves 4

*Roasting Peppers: Cut the peppers in half and place them cut side down on a cookie sheet.

Roast at 375°F (190°C) until the skins are black OR place them under the broiler until the skins are blackened and blistered. The broiler will take less time, but watch carefully.

Place the blackened peppers in a large bowl and cover. This steams them and the skins slip right off after 10 to 15 minutes.

Do not wash the roasted peppers – you will be washing away some of the flavour.

Roasted red peppers have an intense rich flavour that is absolutely delicious. Barb Brattain adds sambuca to her soup recipe to make it really special.

BARB IS EVERYBODY'S *friend. She knocks herself out "doing" for all sorts of people, especially the sick or the halt, or the lame, or the kids or the elderly – even the forests. She is small in stature, but has a very large heart of pure gold!*

Russian Borscht

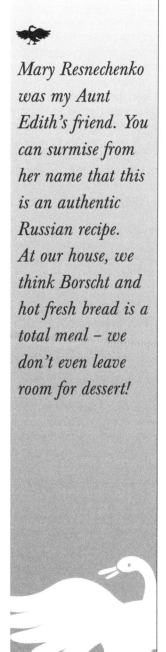

Mary Resnechenko was my Aunt Edith's friend. You can surmise from her name that this is an authentic Russian recipe. At our house, we think Borscht and hot fresh bread is a total meal – we don't even leave room for dessert!

½ cup *(125 mL)* flour
pinch of salt
1 chicken, cut up
4 tbsp. *(60 mL)* olive oil
water
salt and pepper to taste
1 onion, chopped, sautéed
1 red chili pepper, minced
1 large onion, chopped
3 carrots, cubed
3 potatoes, cubed
2 cups *(500 mL)* cooked, cubed beets
½ tsp *(2 mL)* baking soda
4 cups *(1 L)* canned tomatoes
½ small cabbage, shredded
2 sprigs fresh dillweed OR 1 tsp.
    (5 mL) dried
2 cups *(500 mL)* whipping cream
    OR sour cream

Combine the flour and salt. Dredge the chicken in the flour, then brown in the oil in a large saucepan. Cover with water; add salt and pepper to taste and simmer for 2 hours.

Remove the chicken from the broth. Cut the chicken into small pieces, removing the bones and skin. Set aside the meat and discard the bones and skin.

Add the onion to the broth. Add the remaining vegetables in accordance with how long they take to cook. First carrots, then potatoes, add the cooked beets, baking soda and tomatoes. (Add the baking soda before the tomatoes so the cream won't curdle.) Add the shredded cabbage last, to just barely cook it. Put a large handful of fresh dillweed on top, if you have it. Season to taste and add the chicken. Heat through.

Just before serving, add the cream. Just simmer, barely heating through. Discard the dill before you serve the soup. You may alternatively serve the sweet cream or sour cream as side dishes.

Serves 8

Pictured on page 69.

MARY SERVED *this borscht as a soup before a meal. (It was necessary to have been engaging in a lot of physical activity to be able to manage both.) There was always a wonderful dessert and coffee to follow. I have to remind myself that we did burn up a lot of calories every day. We walked everyplace we went and carried our books, groceries, parcels or kids. Walking miles daily was part of life. I mention this as a reasons why we could accept Mary's hospitality without turning into blimps.*

Lebanese Lentil Soup

2 cups *(500 mL)* lentils
salt to taste
6 cups *(1.5 L)* water
1 tbsp. *(15 mL)* olive oil
1 cup *(250 mL)* diced onion
1 cup *(250 mL)* diced carrot
1 cup *(250 mL)* diced celery
1 cup *(250 mL)* diced peppers
2 garlic cloves, minced
1 bay leaf
1 tbsp. *(15 mL)* paprika
1 tsp. *(5 mL)* ground cumin
1 tsp. *(5 mL)* ground coriander
2 tsp. *(10 mL)* ground oregano
1 tsp. *(5 mL)* celery seed
10 cracked peppercorns
1 tbsp. *(15 mL)* dried basil
1 tbsp. *(15 mL)* dried parsley
1 tbsp. *(15 mL)* chopped chives
6 cups *(1.5 L)* chicken stock
2 tbsp. *(30 mL)* Worcestershire sauce
1 cup *(250 mL)* sour cream

Wash the lentils. In a large saucepan, bring the lentils, salt and water to a boil and simmer for 2 to 3 hours, or until the lentils are tender. Drain the lentils and discard the cooking water.

Heat the oil in a frying pan and sauté the vegetables, herbs and spices for 5 minutes. Add the vegetables and stock to the lentils and simmer for about 20 minutes.

Add the Worcestershire. Adjust the seasoning. (That last phrase really means – "Taste it and see if it needs anything.")

A spoonful of sour cream on each serving, adds both flavour and eye appeal.

Serves 8 to 10

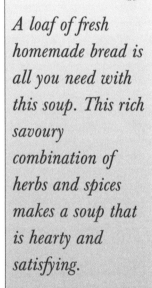

A loaf of fresh homemade bread is all you need with this soup. This rich savoury combination of herbs and spices makes a soup that is hearty and satisfying.

Variations: If you love the tang of fresh lemon juice, make a ***Lebanese Lemon Lentil Soup*** by adding the juice of 3 to 4 lemons and 1 tbsp. (15 mL) of grated lemon rind to this recipe. Other options include sautéed, diced spicy Italian or Greek sausage or cooked diced chicken.

Manhattan Clam Chowder

This soup has great flavour and beautiful colour. I can/preserve my own tomatoes, see page 193, and they add wonderful flavour to this recipe. If you don't have the time or inclination, commercially canned tomatoes are fine, but treat yourself to the real thing sometime.

2 tbsp. *(30 mL)* vegetable oil
1 cup *(250 mL)* finely diced onion
1 cup *(250 mL)* finely diced celery
4 cups *(1 L)* canned tomatoes
2, 5 oz. *(142 g)* cans of baby clams
3, 8 oz. *(250 mL)* bottles clam juice
1 cup *(250 mL)* finely diced carrots
2 cups *(500 mL)* diced potatoes
6 slices bacon, cooked crisp,
    crumbled
1 tsp. *(5 mL)* salt
pepper to taste
½ tsp. *(2 mL)* thyme

In a large saucepan, heat the oil and sauté the onions and celery, then add the tomatoes, the juice from the clams, the clam juice, carrots and potatoes. Add water if needed. Simmer until the carrots and potatoes are just tender.

Add the clams, crumbled bacon, salt, pepper and thyme. Cook for 2 to 3 minutes, just to heat through. Taste and adjust the seasonings.

Serves 6

It is impossible to enjoy cooking if you do not have the necessary equipment – to cut down on the labour. Everyone needs a good electric mixer, food processor, regular blender as well as the handheld blender, decent stainless steel bowls of various sizes, good frying pans as well as good pots and saucepans. Don't forget the whisks, spatulas etc. etc. etc. Buy good ones and look after them. A double boiler is a must in any kitchen – the 2-quart (2 L) size is versatile.

Navy (White) Bean & Sausage Soup

2 lbs. *(1 kg)* white beans

2 ham bones, 4-5" *(10-13 cm)* in length

2 large onions, chopped

1 green pepper, chopped

4 stalks celery, chopped

2 tbsp. *(30 mL)* chopped parsley

2 tsp. *(10 mL)* minced garlic

1 lb. *(500 g)* baked ham, cut into 1" *(2.5 cm)* cubes

salt and pepper to taste

¼ tsp. *(1 mL)* cayenne

¼ tsp. *(1 mL)* ground thyme

2 bay leaves

¼ tsp. *(1 mL)* dried basil

3 qts. *(2.8 L)* water, or more as is needed

6 Creole (smoked) sausages

Wash the beans and soak overnight in cold water to cover. Drain the soaked beans in a colander.

Put the beans, along with all of the other ingredients, except the sausages, in a heavy 10-quart (10 L) pot. Bring to a boil over high heat, then the lower heat and simmer for 3 hours, until beans are tender. Stir from time to time and scrape the sides and bottom of the pot to prevent scorching. Add more water as is needed, when mixture begins to appear dry.

While the beans are cooking, pan-grill the sausages, turning frequently, for about 15 minutes, until cooked through. Drain on paper towel. Slice into ½" (1.3 cm) pieces. Add the sausages to the beans 2 hours into the simmering time. Remember to discard the ham bones and bay leaves before you serve the soup.

Hearty and satisfying, this soup is perfect after a hard day's work or a hard day's skiing. It also freezes and travels well.

Serves 12

Variations: For a ***Pepper & Sausage Bean Soup***, add 2 cups (500 mL) diced, sautéed red peppers to the soup just before serving. Use spicy Italian, Greek or Polish sausage.

Oxtail Soup

This soup is tasty beyond belief!! When you buy oxtail today, it is usually beef tail – but is is still very flavourful. Sherry is the traditional flavouring for this soup, but red wine adds lovely body and colour.

Oxtail Stock:
6 lbs. *(2.5 kg)* oxtail (it will already be cut up for you)
2 medium onions, sliced
2 medium carrots, sliced
bouquet garni*
3 qts. *(2.8 L)* beef broth OR water

Soup Finale:
½ cup *(125 mL)* barley
½ cup *(125 mL)* red wine
2 onions, finely chopped
2 carrots, finely chopped
½ small turnip, finely chopped

Put the oxtail in a roasting pan and pop it into a 400°F (200°C) oven to brown, about 45 minutes. When browned, add the onions, carrots, bouquet garni, broth or water. Simmer for 2 hours, either on top of the stove or in the oven. You will have to add water from time to time.

Remove the stock from the heat. Strain the stock into another pot. Throw away the vegetables and bones, but reserve the meat from the bones. Break the meat into shreds about ¼ x 1" (1 x 10 cm), set aside.

Add the barley and the wine to the stock. Cook only until the barley is almost tender, about 40 minutes.

Add the fresh vegetables and cook for 15 more minutes, until the carrots and turnip are tender. Put the meat back in the pot, bring the soup up to the desired heat and serve.

Serves 6

* Bouquet garni is a tied bunch of herbs, often parsley, bay leaf and thyme, used to add flavour to soups and stews. The herbs are tied for easy removal before serving.

Turkey Noodle Soup

Turkey Stock:
1 turkey carcass
1 large onion, chopped
2 carrots, cubed
4 stalks celery and leaves
salt to taste
water to cover

homemade noodles – use half of
   the Pasta Dough recipe on page
   82

1 onion, finely chopped
3 stalks celery, finely chopped
2 carrots, shredded
leftover turkey, cubed
salt and pepper
fresh homemade noodles

Remove the meat from the turkey bones and cut the meat into small pieces. Set the meat aside. Break the turkey carcass into pieces to fit into a large stock pot. Add the onion, carrots, celery and salt. Cover with water, and bring to a boil.

Skim off the foam and discard. Simmer for 2 to 3 hours.

Strain the soup, keeping the stock and turkey meat and discarding the bones and vegetables.

Make the pasta noodles while the stock is simmering.

Place the fresh vegetables, and turkey meat into the stock, adjust the seasoning and simmer for 15 to 20 minutes, until the vegetables are almost done.

Add the noodles and simmer until the noodles are done, 3 to 4 minutes only for fresh noodles. We like our noodles al dente – you may want them cooked a little more. The decision is yours.

Serves 6 to 8

Granny Olsen's Turkey soup was always made with fresh noodles – there is a difference. However, if you are time-stressed, or totally intimidated by the thought of making your own noodles, make this soup and use spaghetti or fettuccine noodles.

Basic Beef Stock

Homemade stock does make a difference in soups, sauce, etc. Don't feel guilty if you don't have time to make homemade stocks on a regular basis, but do try them when you have some time.

6 lbs. *(2.7 kg)* beef soup bones –
  cut in pieces
1-2 large onions, sliced
6 stalks celery, chopped
1 large bay leaf
4 sprigs parsley
8 whole peppercorns
4 whole cloves
4 whole allspice
salt to taste
2-3 carrots, cubed

In a large stock pot, cover the bones with cold water and bring to a boil. Skim off foam and discard. Add the vegetables and simmer for 2 to 3 hours.

Cool the stock and strain it. Discard the bones and vegetables.

You are now ready to start your soup, or put the stock in the freezer, to be used another time.

For a totally different flavour try browning the bones. It makes a **Brown Stock** with a richer, darker colour and a deeper flavour. Put the bones in a large roasting pan so that they have a lot of room. Place in a 400°F (200°C) oven and roast the bones until they are brown.

Now revert to the stock method described above, covering the bones with cold water and bringing them to a boil.

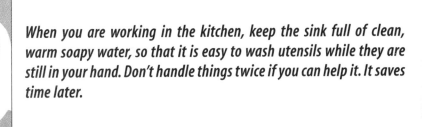

When you are working in the kitchen, keep the sink full of clean, warm soapy water, so that it is easy to wash utensils while they are still in your hand. Don't handle things twice if you can help it. It saves time later.

Salads
&
Vegetables

Caesar Salad

Chef Caesar Cardini's 1924 creation of this salad has inspired restaurants and homemakers across North America to create their own versions. This is our favourite.

1½ cups *(375 mL)* cubed bread
⅓ cup *(75 mL)* melted butter
1 garlic clove, minced
1 large head romaine lettuce, washed and torn into pieces

Caesar Dressing:
1-2 garlic cloves, minced
3 fillets of anchovy (optional)
¾ tsp. *(3 mL)* salt
½ tsp. *(2 mL)* black pepper
⅛ tsp. *(0.5 mL)* dry mustard
½ tsp. *(2 mL)* Worcestershire sauce
few drops Tabasco
½ cup *(125 mL)* olive oil
3 tbsp. *(45 mL)* red wine vinegar
1 lemon, juice of
1 egg, coddled*

8 bacon slices, fried until crisp, crumbled
4 tbsp. *(45 mL)* Parmesan cheese

Prepare the croûtons ahead. Sauté the bread cubes in butter and garlic.

Tear up the lettuce and refrigerate.

I used to do the dressing by hand, in a bowl with a fork or a whisk, but in this day and age of wonderful machinery – it is easier to use a food processor or blender. Use the same sequence or order, garlic, anchovies, salt, pepper, mustard, Worcestershire, Tabasco, and a bit of the olive oil. Blend to a smooth paste.

Add the vinegar and lemon juice. Add the remaining oil slowly, with the blender running. Last of all, blend in the egg.

When it is time to serve, drizzle the dressing over the lettuce and toss well. Add croûtons, bacon bits and Parmesan and toss once more.

Serves 4 to 6

*For health reasons, it is advisable to coddle the egg. To coddle, place the egg in a cup filled with boiling water. Let stand for 1 to 2 minutes.

Pictured on page 105.

Greek Salad

2 large ripe tomatoes
1 cucumber
¼ purple onion
2 tsp. *(10 mL)* red wine vinegar
⅓ cup *(75 mL)* virgin olive oil
salt and pepper to taste
½ tsp. *(2 mL)* oregano
½-¾ cup *(125-175 mL)* cubed feta
    cheese (goat feta is the best)
6 black olives (if you are Greek
    then you will need 12)

Cut the tomatoes in wedges or slices. Slice the cucumber. Thinly slice the onion. Place the vegetables in a salad bowl. Drizzle with vinegar and olive oil. Add salt to taste. Sprinkle with oregano.

Crumble the cheese and sprinkle over the salad. Toss the salad, mixing well.

Arrange the olives on top. Allow the vegetables to marinate for a few minutes before serving.

Serve this salad with a crusty baguette to dunk into and soak up the juices.

Serves 2

Pictured on page 69.

Variations: *Salata Horiatiki,* or Greek Country-Style/Village Salads, include tomatoes, feta, Kalamata olives and cucumbers as the basic ingredients, but fresh seasonal ingredients are also added as they are available, including green peppers, red or white onions, and sometimes shredded cabbage or lettuce, even capers or anchovies.

Lemon juice is often used instead of vinegar, or sometimes olive oil is the only dressing.

Katina Martin, my daughter-in-law, loves Greek Salad. (Who doesn't?) She has been accused of serving it at every meal. Not true. She misses breakfast – at least when we visit.

Four Bean &
Chickpea Salad

My cousin Dian Beach makes an awesome bean salad. The chickpeas add the crunch and the herbed vinaigrette adds punch. No picnic or barbecue is complete without this great take-along.

19 oz. *(540 mL)* can green beans
19 oz. *(540 mL)* can wax beans
19 oz. *(540 mL)* can red (kidney) beans
19 oz. *(540 mL)* can lima beans
19 oz. *(540 mL)* can chickpeas (garbanzo beans)
1 onion, thinly sliced
1 pepper, thinly sliced

Herbed Red Wine Vinaigrette
½ cup *(125 mL)* sugar
½ cup *(125 mL)* olive oil
½ cup *(125 mL)* red wine vinegar
salt and pepper to taste
½ tsp. *(2 mL)* dry mustard
1 tsp. *(5 mL)* tarragon
1 tsp. *(5 mL)* dried basil
2 tbsp. *(30 mL)* chopped parsley

Drain off and discard all of the liquid from each can of beans and the chickpeas. Place the drained beans and chickpeas in a large bowl. Stir in the onions and peppers.

Combine all of the vinaigrette ingredients. Mix well. Add to the salad and mix well.

Refrigerate overnight. It's as simple as that!

Serves 16 to 18

WHEN *Dian was two, her dad developed pneumonia and very nearly died. (No antibiotics in those days.) Mom went to Maple Creek to nurse Uncle Eugene and Granny brought Dian to our place so she could look after her during this very stressful time.*

Granny loved all animals but felt very strongly that they absolutely should not be in the house! Well, in spite of her disapproval, we had not only a live-in dog, but also a cat. To accommodate these furry members of our family we kept a dish of water on the floor.

Granny and Dian settled in, and things were going along very smoothly, in spite of the fact that Dian was a normal busy two-year-old. One day, Granny was sitting in the living room, reading the paper, when she realized that Dian was not only quiet, but out of sight. Quick investigation revealed Dian sitting on the kitchen floor beside the water dish, dipping Granny's toothbrush in the water and scrubbing her baby teeth with great vigor and enthusiasm! Granny was galvanized into action. It was good to have something to laugh about at such a stressful time in our lives.

SOUP, BREAD & SALAD

Russian Borscht, page 58

Irish Soda Bread, page 15

Greek Salad, page 67

Macaroni-Pimiento Salad

3 cups *(750 mL)* uncooked elbow
   macaroni
1 tsp. *(2 mL)* salt
½ cup *(125 mL)* chopped pimiento
1 cup *(250 mL)* finely chopped celery
½ cup *(125 mL)* finely chopped
   green onions
4 hard-boiled eggs
1 cup *(250 mL)* mayonnaise
¼ cup *(60 mL)* sweet pickle juice
¼ tsp. *(1 mL)* paprika
salt and pepper to taste
1 tsp. *(5 mL)* chopped parsley

Savoury Additions:
shrimp
smoked salmon
chicken
avocado
tuna
curry powder
grated cheese

Cook the macaroni in boiling salted water. Drain and cool. Add the celery, pimiento and onion. Add 2 diced hard-boiled eggs.

Add any or a combination of the savoury additions listed.

Combine the mayonnaise, pickle juice and paprika, stir into the macaroni. Add salt and pepper to taste.

Slice the remaining 2 hard-boiled eggs and use for garnish.

Garnish with parsley.

Refrigerate the salad until ready to serve.

Taste the salad just before serving it and adjust the seasoning.

Serves 12 to 14

Many macaroni salads are very bland. Cooling the pasta before adding the dressing is very important. Undercooking the pasta and rinsing the hot pasta with cold water enhances the texture for salads.

If you need a quick vinaigrette, mix three parts oil to one part vinegar in a jar with a lid; shake like blazes. You could also use four parts oil to one part fresh lemon juice. Of course, I favour olive oil, raspberry vinegar and a good-looking lemon.

Honeyed Waldorf Salad
— with Variations

This salad has been popular since the 1890s when it originated at the Waldorf-Astoria Hotel in New York. Granny Olsen's version adds walnuts, cream and a taste of honey to the original.

2 cups *(500 mL)* diced apples
2 tbsp. *(30 mL)* lemon juice
1 cup *(250 mL)* chopped celery
½ cup *(125 mL)* chopped walnuts
¼ cup *(60 mL)* mayonnaise
2 tbsp. *(30 mL)* light cream
2 tbsp. *(30 mL)* honey

Dice the apples and drizzle them with lemon juice — to keep the colour bright.

Chop the celery and nuts and combine with the apples.

Mix the mayonnaise, cream and honey and add to the apple mixture. Toss well.

Serves 6

Variations: Add any of the following ingredients to vary the flavour and texture of this salad:
  cooked chicken pieces
  halved grapes
  orange sections
  grapefruit sections
  raisins

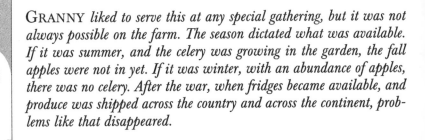

GRANNY *liked to serve this at any special gathering, but it was not always possible on the farm. The season dictated what was available. If it was summer, and the celery was growing in the garden, the fall apples were not in yet. If it was winter, with an abundance of apples, there was no celery. After the war, when fridges became available, and produce was shipped across the country and across the continent, problems like that disappeared.*

24-Hour Ambrosia

2 eggs
3 tbsp. *(45 mL)* lemon juice
4 tbsp. *(60 mL)* sugar
1 tbsp. *(15 mL)* butter
1 cup *(250 mL)* whipping cream, whipped
19 oz. *(540 mL)* can fruit cocktail, drained
14 oz. *(398 mL)* can crushed pine-apple, drained
10 oz. *(284 mL)* can orange segments, drained
¾ of a 14 oz. *(400 g)* pkg. large marshmallows, cut up
½ cup *(125 mL)* chopped maraschino cherries

In the top of a double boiler, combine and beat together the eggs, lemon juice, sugar and butter. Heat, stirring constantly, until thick and smooth.

When the dressing is cool, add the whipped cream, the drained fruit, marshmallows and cherries.

Place in a clear glass serving bowl. Refrigerate for 24 hours before serving.

Serves 8 to 10

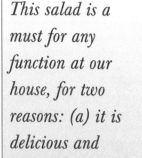

This salad is a must for any function at our house, for two reasons: (a) it is delicious and everyone loves it, (b) it can be made the day ahead.

Beet Salad

16 oz. *(450 g)* can beets
3 oz. *(85 g)* pkg. lemon Jell-o
⅓ cup *(75 mL)* sugar
⅓ cup *(75 mL)* vinegar
1½ tbsp. *(22 mL)* horseradish
2 tsp. *(10 mL)* lemon juice
few drops of Tabasco
4 oz. *(125 g)* pkg. cream cheese
2 tbsp. *(30 mL)* mayonnaise

lettuce leaves

Drain the beets. Save the liquid and add enough water to the beet juice to make 1½ cups (375 mL). Bring the beet liquid to a boil and add the Jell-o. Stir until dissolved. Add the sugar, vinegar, horseradish, lemon juice and Tabasco.

Shred or slice the beets into shoe-string size. Add the beets to the Jell-o mixture and pour into a 9" (23 cm) square glass pan. Refrigerate until set.

When ready to serve, combine the cream cheese and mayonnaise. Spread the cheese mixture over the the Beet Salad. Cut in fairly small squares and serve on lettuce leaves.

Serves 9

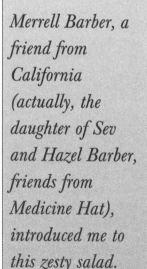

Merrell Barber, a friend from California (actually, the daughter of Sev and Hazel Barber, friends from Medicine Hat), introduced me to this zesty salad.

Lime Vegetable Salad

I know that jellied salads are not considered "cookbook fare", but for many, many families this creamy salad, filled with crunchy vegetables, is the highlight of a holiday dinner.

3 oz. *(85 g)* pkg. lime Jell-o
1 cup *(250 mL)* boiling water
¾ cup *(175 mL)* mayonnaise
1 cup *(250 mL)* creamed cottage cheese
½ cup *(125 mL)* chopped celery
¼ cup *(60 mL)* chopped red pepper
1 cup *(250 mL)* shredded cabbage
1 apple, chopped
1 carrot, shredded
1 small onion, chopped.

In a large bowl, mix the boiling water with the Jell-o. Stir until the Jell-o is completely dissolved.

Add the mayonnaise and beat until smooth. Add the prepared vegetables and stir thoroughly.

Pour into a glass serving dish and refrigerate overnight.

Serves 8

MOM *was a wonderful mother, with many good qualities and talents, but cooking was not one of them. She was not a cook and never pretended to be. However, for some reason, every year she felt duty bound to make this salad for our Christmas Dinner.*

Without fail – she forgot to put it on the table, which meant we were eating it the next day, with leftover turkey. (It really makes more sense to have it with cold turkey anyway.) We loved her special salad but, being human, we could not resist teasing her by calling it her Boxing Day Salad.

Scalloped Potatoes

½ cup *(125 mL)* chopped onion
4 tbsp. *(60 mL)* butter, melted
3 tbsp. *(45 mL)* flour
salt and pepper to taste
3 cups *(750 mL)* milk
8 cups *(2 L)* thinly sliced potatoes
½ cup *(125 mL)* shredded cheese
   (optional)

Butter a 3-quart (3 L) ovenproof casserole.

Put the onion, butter, flour, salt, pepper and milk in a blender and mix thoroughly.

Arrange the potato slices in the buttered casserole and pour the milk mixture over the potatoes.

Cover and bake at 350°F (180°C) for 45 minutes. Uncover and bake for 20 minutes. If using, sprinkle with cheese and bake for 5 more minutes.

Serves 6

Variations: Some versions use chicken broth or cream rather than milk. Grated Parmesan or Cheddar cheese may be layered between the potatoes. Crushed garlic may be added to the sauce.

Another classic, community and church fowl/fall suppers and festive family gatherings have been graced with scalloped potatoes for many decades. Every family has their favourite version.

Bacon & Sausage Layered Potatoes

2 lbs. *(1 kg)* new potatoes
4 hard-boiled eggs, sliced
7 oz. *(200 g)* spicy sausage, sliced
1¼ cups *(300 mL)* sour cream
8 oz. *(225 g)* bacon, cooked crisp, crumbled
2 tbsp. *(30 mL)* bread crumbs

Cook the potatoes in their skins in boiling salted water. Drain and leave to cool until just warm. Peel and slice the potatoes.

Butter a 3-quart (3 L) ovenproof casserole. Cover the bottom of the dish with a layer of sliced potato; add a layer of egg and sausage. Pour over a generous layer of sour cream, adding a sprinkle of bacon.

Continue the layers. Reserve some sour cream and bacon for the last layer. Sprinkle bread crumbs on top.

Bake at 350°F (180°C) for 40 minutes, until the top is crisp and browned.

Serves 4 to 6

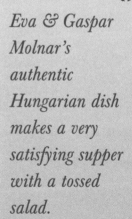

Eva & Gaspar Molnar's authentic Hungarian dish makes a very satisfying supper with a tossed salad.

Special Mashed Potatoes

This is the potato recipe used at our house when we have a sit-down dinner for 12 to 14 people. It calls for 10 large potatoes – I generally use the rule of one potato per adult and one for the pot, not counting the young children, and adjust the recipe accordingly. Making the potatoes a day ahead certainly cuts down on the work and kitchen confusion the day of the dinner.

10 large potatoes, peeled, chunked
1 tsp. *(5 mL)* salt
½ cup *(125 mL)* cream
½ cup *(125 mL)* butter
8 oz. *(250 g)* pkg. cream cheese
½ cup *(125 mL)* sour cream
1 tsp. *(5 mL)* onion salt
salt to taste
white pepper to taste
milk to adjust consistency, if
   necessary
paprika

Cook the potatoes in a large pot, in salted water, until tender. Drain.

Mash* the potatoes until they are smooth and creamy. Add the cream, butter, cream cheese, sour cream, onion salt, salt and pepper. If they are too stiff, add a little milk or cream.

Pour the mashed potatoes into a buttered 3-quart (3 L) ovenproof casserole. Allow them to cool. Cover and refrigerate.

Take the potatoes out of the refrigerator 1 to 2 hours before placing them in the oven.

Sprinkle the potatoes with paprika and bake, uncovered, at 350°F (180°C) for 30 to 40 minutes.

Serves 10 to 12

* To mash the potatoes, use a potato masher. A food processor will break down the potato texture to a gluey mass. Warming the cream or milk and butter before adding them to the potatoes will give a better mashed texture.

Note: Baking potatoes have a low moisture and high starch content. Their mealy texture is best for mashed potatoes. Russet/Idaho and Yukon Gold potatoes are excellent for mashed potatoes.

Hash-Brown Potatoes

3 large potatoes
1-2 tbsp. *(15-30 mL)* **minced onion**
salt and pepper to taste
¼ cup *(60 mL)* **butter**

Partly boil the potatoes, then cool. Peel the potatoes and shred, using a medium shredder.

Combine potatoes and onion and season.

Heat a 9" (23 cm) cast-iron frying pan. Melt the butter and pat the potato mixture into the pan, leaving ½" (1.3 cm) around the edge. Cover the potatoes with a flat lid that also is ½" (1.3 cm) smaller than the pan. Lower the heat and cook for 5 minutes.

When the bottom of the potato cake has turned a nice brown, cut the cake in quarters and turn 1 quarter at a time with a spatula OR place a large plate over the frying pan and invert the potato cake onto the plate. Slide the uncooked side into the pan; cover again with the lid and cook for another 5 minutes, until browned.

A properly seasoned cast-iron frying pan is the secret here.

Also, the lid is important. At almost any kitchen shop you can buy flat, glass 8" (20 cm) lids, that are perfect for making hash browns in a 9" (23 cm) pan.

Serves 4

Note: There are four basic potato categories: russet, long white, round red and round white. The round red and round white are better for boiling than for baking as their waxy flesh is more moist and has less starch than the russet or long white, which are better for baking. Yukon Gold fits into the boiling potato category.

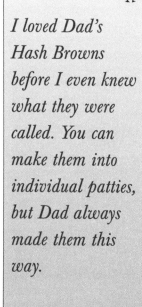

I loved Dad's Hash Browns before I even knew what they were called. You can make them into individual patties, but Dad always made them this way.

Sweet Potato and Pineapple Soufflé

This is my granddaughter Tracey's special-occasion sweet potato dish.

4 egg whites
2 cups *(500 mL)* mashed sweet
    potatoes
6 tbsp. *(90 mL)* brown sugar
¼ cup *(60 mL)* milk
2 tsp. *(10 mL)* cornstarch
¼ tsp. *(1 mL)* cinnamon
pinch of nutmeg
¼ tsp. *(1 mL)* vanilla

Pineapple Brown Sugar Topping:
½ cup *(125 mL)* dark brown
    (Demerara) sugar
4 tbsp. *(60 mL)* butter
2 tbsp. *(30 mL)* flour
14 oz. *(398 mL)* can crushed
    pineapple, drained

Beat the egg whites until stiff. Set aside.

In a separate bowl, beat the sweet potatoes with the sugar. Add the milk, cornstarch, spices and vanilla. Fold the potato mixture into egg whites and mix thoroughly.

Pour into a greased 2-quart (2 L) casserole.

Topping: Heat the butter and brown sugar in a microwave for 30 to 40 seconds, just until melted.

Stir in the flour, until there are no lumps. Stir the drained pineapple into the butter mixture. Drizzle evenly over the sweet potatoes.

Bake at 350°F (180°C) for 30 to 35 minutes, until golden brown and bubbly on top. Serve immediately.

Serves 4

Pictured on the front cover.

TRACEY *has liked cooking since she was a little girl. If she was around when I baked bread, she would pull up a chair so that she could help punch down the dough. She always had to form her own loaf. Her mom, Judy, always laughingly referred to Tracey as a throwback to our side of the family. I happily accepted the compliment.*

Nut-Crusted Squash

1 Hubbard squash
½ cup *(125 mL)* melted butter
¼ cup *(75 mL)* finely chopped
  peanuts
⅓ cup *(75 mL)* crushed Rice Krispies
⅓ cup *(75 mL)* light brown sugar

Wash the squash and cut it in half. Remove the seeds. Cut the squash into 3" (8 cm) cubes. Place in a shallow cookie pan, skin side up, with ⅓" (1 cm) of water.

Bake at 350°F (180°C) for 45 minutes.

Cool and peel the squash.

Combine the nuts, Rice Krispies and sugar in a shallow pan.

Roll the squash cubes in melted butter, then roll them in the nut mixture. Arrange on a cookie sheet.

Cover the squash with foil for the first 5 minutes. Bake at 400°F (200°C) for 15 minutes.

Serves 6 to 8

This is a recipe many people would pass over as "ho hum" – in fact it is surprisingly tasty.

Parsnip Cakes

5 parsnips, cooked and mashed
2 tbsp. *(30 mL)* flour
pinch of salt
pinch of pepper
1 tbsp. *(15 mL)* chopped onion
1 egg, slightly beaten
½ cup *(125 mL)* cracker crumbs
2 tbsp. *(30 mL)* butter

Combine the parsnips, flour, salt, pepper, onion and egg.

Form the parsnip mixture into patties and coat the patties with the cracker crumbs.

Fry in butter until browned.

Serves 4

Parsnips have a slightly sweet, slightly spicy flavour. Cooked parsnips have a velvety, potato-like texture.

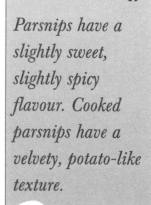

Red Cabbage with Red Wine, Apples, Prunes and Apricots

Keep the wine bottle handy in case it needs more moisture. This is the perfect companion to Rouladen.

2 large red onions, finely chopped
½ cup *(125 mL)* olive oil
8 carrots, grated
1 large red cabbage, finely shredded
1 cup *(250 mL)* finely chopped prunes
1 cup *(250 mL)* finely chopped dried apricots
1 large apple, peeled and sliced
4 lemons, juice of
3 oranges, juice of
3 tbsp. *(45 mL)* sugar
1½ cups *(375 mL)* red wine
1 tsp. *(5 mL)* pepper
3 tsp. *(15 mL)* caraway seeds (optional)

In a very large saucepan, sauté the onions in oil until translucent.

Add carrots, cabbage, prunes, apricots, apple, juices, sugar, wine, pepper and caraway seeds. Stir well and cover tightly. Bring heat up for a few minutes, then turn to low and cook for 1½ hours.

Watch that this does not burn. I am inclined to put it in the oven for that reason, but you still have to watch it.

Serves 8 to 10

Baked Beans

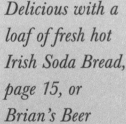

Delicious with a loaf of fresh hot Irish Soda Bread, page 15, or Brian's Beer Bread, page 16.

1 lb. *(500 g)* white beans
1 ham bone
1 large onion, chopped
1½ tsp. *(7 mL)* salt
½ tsp. *(2 mL)* pepper
2 tsp. *(10 mL)* vinegar
½ tsp. *(2 mL)* mustard
2 tbsp. *(30 mL)* brown sugar
¼ cup *(60 mL)* molasses
¼ cup *(60 mL)* ketchup
4 cups *(1 L)* canned tomatoes

Wash the beans well and soak overnight in water to cover.

In the morning, drain the beans and add fresh water to cover. Add the ham bone and boil for 30 minutes. (Skim off foam and discard.) Take the beans off the heat and allow them to sit, uncovered, for 30 minutes.

Add the remaining ingredients and bake at 250°F (120°C) for 6 hours, or until the beans are tender. Add water as is necessary.

Serves 8

Main Course Dishes

Pasta Dough

We could always count on having turkey noodle soup a couple of days after the turkey dinner, to me that was the best part. Granny Olsen always thought that if you used only yolks you would have a more tender noodle, if you find yourself with a cupful of yolks someday, you might want to experiment.

6 eggs
2 tbsp. *(30 mL)* olive oil
1 tsp. *(5 mL)* salt
3 cups *(750 mL)* flour

Place the eggs in a large mixing bowl. Add the salt and oil and beat with an electric mixer. Slowly add the flour.

The secret to this is to know when the dough is just right. You don't want it too stiff to handle, but you don't want it so sloppy that it is too sticky to manage. If it seems sticky, sprinkle flour on the counter and knead the dough, as you would bread dough, until it is no longer sticky.

With a rolling pin, roll out the dough until it is very thin. Roll up the noodle dough as you would a cinnamon roll, then cut the noodles the thickness you like. Thick noodles, thin noodles, lasagne noodles, the sky is the limit with this recipe.

If you have a noodle maker it is not necessary to do the rolling process. The noodle maker is a wonderful invention.

Yield: noodles for approximately 8 to 10

Note: Commercial dried pasta is usually made with durum wheat flour (semolina) and water, or milk. Fresh pasta is usually made with unbleached all-purpose flour, whole eggs or egg whites, water or wine and sometimes a spoonful of olive oil and minced fresh herbs.

Pastas may be coloured with spinach, tomato paste, beet juice or squid ink. Egg noodles are often enriched with egg yolks. They can be made with whole eggs and/or egg yolks.

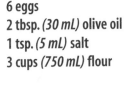

Deluxe Lasagne

pasta dough, page 82, cut into
    lasagne noodles

Cream Sauce:
2 cups *(500 mL)* milk
2 egg yolks
2 tbsp. *(30 mL)* butter
2 tbsp. *(30 mL)* flour

Meat Sauce:
2 tbsp. *(30 mL)* butter
1 chicken breast, ground
6 oz. *(170 g)* ground lean pork
6 oz. *(170 g)* ground lean veal
6 oz. *(170 g)* Italian sausage, diced
1 tbsp. *(15 mL)* dried rosemary
salt and pepper to taste
½ cup *(125 mL)* Parmesan cheese
pinch of nutmeg
pinch of cinnamon
2, 10 oz. *(283 g)* pkgs. spinach,
    thawed, chopped, drained

Tomato Sauce:
¼ cup *(60 mL)* olive oil
¼ cup *(60 mL)* butter
1 onion, chopped
1 garlic clove
2 carrots, shredded
3 stalks celery, minced
pinch of dried sweet basil
5½ oz. *(156 mL)* can tomato paste
4 lbs. *(2 kg)* fresh tomatoes, chopped
salt and pepper to taste

½ lb. *(250 g)* mozzarella, sliced
½ cup *(125 mL)* grated Parmesan

Prepare the noodles, then prepare the sauces before you cook the noodles.

Cream sauce: Combine the milk and eggs. Melt the butter; stir in the flour then milk, until smooth. Set aside.

Meat sauce: Melt the butter and sauté the chicken, pork, veal and sausage, one at a time. Put the meats into a large bowl as they are cooked. Stir in the rosemary, salt, pepper, Parmesan, nutmeg, cinnamon and spinach. Set aside.

Tomato sauce: Heat the oil and butter and sauté the onion and garlic. Add the carrots, celery, basil, tomato paste, tomatoes and salt and pepper to taste; simmer until the sauce is thickened, about 20 minutes.

Cook the noodles.

Grease an 11 x 15 x 3" (28 x 38 x 8 cm) pan. Line it with 1 layer of noodles. Spoon in a layer of meat sauce, then tomato sauce, then cream sauce. Top with a layer of mozzarella then another layer of noodles. Continue until you have used all the ingredients, ending with a cheese layer. Cover lightly with a sheet of foil.

Bake at 400°F (200°C) for 40 minutes. Remove the cover, reduce temperature to 350°F (180°C). Sprinkle with Parmesan and return to the oven until the Parmesan browns.

Serves 12

Pictured on page 105.

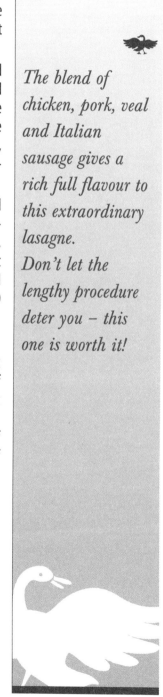

The blend of chicken, pork, veal and Italian sausage gives a rich full flavour to this extraordinary lasagne.
Don't let the lengthy procedure deter you – this one is worth it!

Herbed Tomato &
Beef Spaghetti Sauce

Slow cooking develops the hearty satisfying flavours of this classic pasta sauce.

2 lbs. *(1 kg)* ground round steak OR
   lean ground beef
2 onions, chopped
8 cups *(2 L)* canned tomatoes
1 hot red chili pepper, chopped
½ tsp. *(2 mL)* cinnamon
½ tsp. *(2 mL)* ground oregano
½ tsp. *(2 mL)* ground rosemary
1 tbsp. *(15 mL)* dried parsley
2 tbsp. *(30 mL)* sugar
1 tsp. *(5 mL)* salt
2 cups *(500 mL)* water

In a large saucepan, cook the ground beef and onion until the meat is no longer pink.

Add the remaining ingredients and simmer over very low heat for 4 hours. Watch carefully and stir often. Add water from time to time, as needed.

Serve this sauce over spaghetti, or your favourite pasta shapes.

Serves 6 to 8

Note: There is sometimes confusion between types of peppers. Chili (or chile) peppers come in more than 200 varieties. The general rule is that the smaller the chili pepper the hotter it is. They vary from about 12" (30 cm) to ¼" (1 cm) and can be various shades of red, yellow, green or black. The heat comes from capsaicin which is mostly concentrated in the seeds and membranes.

Sweet peppers include bell peppers and sweet banana peppers. The red bell peppers are ripened green peppers, but bell peppers also come in yellow, orange, brown and purple. Pimientos belong to the sweet pepper group.

Cheddar & Bacon Macaroni Loaf

2 cups *(500 mL)* uncooked macaroni

2 tbsp. *(30 mL)* butter
1 cup *(250 mL)* chopped onion
2 cups *(500 mL)* hot milk
2 cups *(500 mL)* lightly packed
   grated Cheddar cheese
2 tbsp. *(30 mL)* chopped pimiento
2 tbsp. *(30 mL)* chopped parsley
6 eggs, well beaten
8 oz. *(250 g)* Cheddar cheese, sliced

Cheese Sauce:
2 tbsp. *(30 mL)* butter
2 tbsp. *(30 mL)* flour
½ tsp. *(2 mL)* dry mustard
¾ tsp. *(3 mL)* salt
pinch of pepper
2 cups *(500 mL)* milk
½ cup *(125 mL)* grated cheese

3 strips bacon, cooked crisp,
   crumbled
6 strips pimiento
2 tbsp. *(30 mL)* chopped parsley

Cook the macaroni and drain.

In a large saucepan, melt the butter and sauté the onion. Add the hot milk. Stir in the grated cheese. Stir in the pimiento and parsley. Add the cooked macaroni and stir in the eggs. Combine well.

Layer the macaroni mixture and the sliced cheese, making several layers, into a well-greased 5 x 9 x 3" (13 x 23 x 8 cm) loaf pan. Press down fairly firmly.

Bake at 350°F (180°C) for 45 to 55 minutes, watching carefully to make sure it does not get too brown.

Sauce: Melt the butter in a saucepan. Stir in the flour, dry mustard, salt and pepper. Stir in the milk until smooth. Stir in the cheese until smooth. The sauce should be of a pouring consistency.

When the macaroni loaf is cooked, let it sit in the pan for 5 minutes. Turn the loaf out onto a large platter. Pour the sauce over and arrange the crumbled bacon and pimiento on top. Sprinkle parsley around the edges.

Serves 6

This recipe is not only delicious – it has eye appeal!

Puerto Nuevo Fish

This is so delicious that even those that don't like fish will enjoy it! You can vary the type of fish and add shrimp or even crab, as you wish.

Per person:
2 tbsp. *(30 mL)* butter
single portion of fish fillet (red
　　snapper, salmon, etc.)
　　OR 4 jumbo shrimp
1 garlic clove, minced
¼ onion, sliced
1 tomato, sliced
¼ red bell pepper, sliced
2 tbsp. *(30 mL)* cream
¼ tsp. *(1 mL)* minced parsley
1 tbsp. *(15 mL)* white wine
dash Maggi* sauce
2-3 fresh mushrooms, sliced

Spread a sheet of strong aluminum foil with butter and place the fish fillet and/or shrimp on it.

Top the fish with the garlic, onion, tomato, red pepper, cream, parsley, wine, Maggi sauce and sliced mushrooms. Wrap the foil tightly, so that no juices can escape.

Place the foil package on a very hot barbecue grill for 5 minutes. Then make 5 to 6 holes in the top of the foil with a toothpick. Cook for 3 to 4 minutes more.

Remove the foil packet from the heat and open it. Remove the fish from the foil and serve, or eat it right out of the foil.

Serve with rice or crisp rolls to soak up the wonderful juices.

Serves 1

Pictured opposite.

* Available in the spice section of most supermarkets.

ALL OF THE *food at Roberto's Puerto Nuevo Restaurant in Puerto Vallarta is excellent. This is my favourite. Luckily, Roberto shares the recipe readily. It is a wonderful dish made at home, but the ambiance of Puerto Vallarta, the wonderful service at Roberto's, the pleasant Margarita, see page 47, beforehand, all add a certain something to the flavour. Don't miss it.*

MAIN DISHES – FISH

Puerto Nuevo Fish, page 86

Margarita, page 47

Poached Salmon

4 tbsp. *(60 mL)* butter, melted
3 lb. *(1.5 kg)* whole salmon, cleaned, skin intact
1 tsp. *(5 mL)* salt
½ tsp. *(2 mL)* pepper
½ tsp. *(2 mL)* ground thyme
1½ cups *(375 mL)* light cream
1 medium onion, sliced
2 sprigs of fresh parsley
2 garlic cloves, minced
1 large bay leaf

Place the melted butter in a long rectangular baking dish. Dip the salmon in the butter and turn to coat the other side. Rub the salmon with the salt, pepper and thyme. Add the cream, onions, parsley, garlic and bay leaf.

Cover and bake at 350°F (180°C) for about 40 minutes. Baste the fish occasionally with the pan juices.

Discard the vegetables, bay leaf, etc. Remove the bones before serving.

Serve with rice or Special Mashed Potatoes, page 76.

Serves 8 to 10

Traditional salmon poaching uses simmering water, often flavoured with wine, vegetables and herbs. This simmering garlic-flavoured cream adds a rich, comfort-food quality.

Fish Cakes

2 cups *(500 mL)* flaked cooked OR canned salmon
6 crackers, finely crumbled
½ cup *(125 mL)* minced onion
2 tbsp. *(30 mL)* cornmeal
2 eggs, not beaten
½ cup *(125 mL)* whole OR evaporated milk

butter

Combine the salmon and crackers in a medium bowl. Mix in the onion and cornmeal, and then the eggs. Add the milk a little at a time, the mixture must be the right consistency for the patties to hold together.

Form patties and fry in butter, turning to brown both sides.

Serves 4

I like leftover salmon better this way than the first time around.

GRANNY LAKUSTA *is one of those hardworking courageous people that helped settle western Canada. She is over 90 and still going strong. This is just one of her many, many wonderful recipes.*

Salmon with Sautéed Cabbage & Red Pepper

This colourful dish combines the lively flavours of ginger and soy with the mellow flavours of cabbage and salmon. The sauce is tangy with a touch of mustard and horseradish.

Honey Yogurt Horseradish Sauce:

1 cup *(250 mL)* yogurt
1 tsp. *(5 mL)* horseradish, or more to taste
1 tsp. *(5 mL)* prepared mustard
1 tsp. *(5 mL)* honey
few drops Tabasco

3 tbsp. *(45 mL)* olive oil
1 tbsp. *(15 mL)* julienned ginger
1 onion, chopped
2 stalks celery, thinly sliced
1 red pepper, chopped
1 small head of cabbage, chopped
½ tsp. *(2 mL)* salt
½ tsp. *(2 mL)* pepper
2 tsp. *(10 mL)* soy sauce
1 cup *(250 mL)* frozen peas

1½ cups *(375 mL)* cooked salmon*

Prepare the sauce by mixing all of the ingredients in a bowl. Stir well and set aside.

Heat the oil in a large frying pan and add the ginger, onion, celery, red pepper and cabbage. Sauté until the cabbage wilts and cooks down. Stir in the salt, pepper and soy sauce. Add the peas to just barely heat through.

Place the cooked salmon in the centre of a large platter. Place the sautéed cabbage and other vegetables around the outer edge of the platter. Then pour the sauce between the salmon and the cabbage.

Serves 4 to 6

* The salmon may be heated separately, or it may be heated with the cabbage, adding it just before the peas are added. If the salmon is heated with the vegetables, simply pour the sauce over the salmon and the vegetables.

Variations: Substitute cooked tuna or 2 cups (500 mL) home-canned or leftover cooked chicken for the salmon. You may also use leftover cooked salmon.

Rule for baking fish: *Bake at 350°F (180°C) for 10 minutes for each 1" (2.5 cm) of thickness. If it is all or partly frozen you will have to adjust that. Greg gave me a good tip for barbecuing fish of any kind – barbecue it on a piece of lettuce. The lettuce keeps it moist and it is not so apt to crumble. You also don't have the problem of the fish sticking to the grill.*

Roast Goose or Turkey

Sausage Apple Stuffing:
6 cups *(1.5 L)* bread cubes
1 lb. *(500 kg)* pork sausage meat
1½ cups *(375 mL)* chopped onion
1½ cups *(375 mL)* chopped celery
1 apple, cored, chopped
salt and pepper to taste
1 tsp. *(5 mL)* ground savory
¾ cup *(175 mL)* melted butter

chicken broth, orange juice, wine or
   sherry, to moisten

goose OR turkey – approximately
   1 lb. *(450 g)* of goose or turkey
   per person

Stuffing: Place the bread cubes on a cookie sheet and toast in the oven. Place in a large bowl.

Sauté the sausage meat; drain off fat. Combine the sausage with the bread cubes. Sauté the onions and celery; add to bread cubes. Add chopped apple, salt, pepper and savory. Melt the butter and drizzle over the dressing. Mix thoroughly.

If you feel the dressing needs a little more moisture to hold together, add a little broth, orange juice, wine or sherry. (There are no hard and fast rules about dressing, you can put in almost anything you please.)

To prepare the goose or turkey: Remove the pin feathers with tweezers. Make sure all of the insides have been removed.

Wipe the carcass, inside and out, with a cloth soaked in vinegar.

Stuff the neck cavity and pin back the flap. Stuff the main cavity and sew or pin the cavity shut. Tie the legs to the body so that they do not stick up in the air.

Place the bird breast up in an appropriately-sized roasting pan. Do not add water.

Roast at 450°F (230°C) for 20 minutes. At this point, salt the bird and cover it loosely with foil or a lid. Turn the oven down to 325°F (160°C). Roast the stuffed bird for about 30 minutes per pound (500 g)*.

Take the foil off near the end to brown the bird, if it is not already browned.

Let the bird sit for 20 minutes before you carve it.

* Larger birds will take less time per pound to roast. At 325°F (160°C), approximate times are: 6 lbs. (3 kg) – 3 hours; 12 lbs. (5.5 kg) – 3¾ hours; 16 lbs. (7 kg) – 4 hours; 22 lbs. (10 kg) – 4½ hours.

Roast goose was the inspiration for the name of my cookbook. Granny Olsen's recipe works well for both goose and turkey. Her Sausage Apple Stuffing is moist and will stuff a 15 to 20 lb. (7 to 9 kg) bird.

Bread Sauce

Granny Garratt's recipe for Bread Sauce is one of the oldest in this book. It has been in our family for about 120 years. It is an English dish that traditionally accompanies goose or pheasant. Having grown up with it I love it but, I have never been served Bread Sauce anyplace but at our own table. It is not a gourmet dish, but it does for a goose what cranberry sauce does for a turkey.

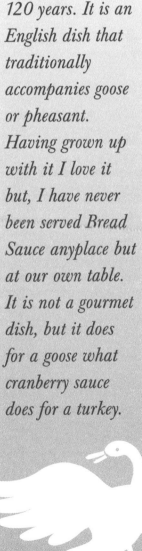

1 cup *(250 mL)* milk
1 small onion, finely chopped
1 bay leaf
4 whole cloves
pinch of salt
pinch of pepper
2-3 slices bread, cubed
¼ tsp. *(1 mL)* nutmeg
2 tbsp. *(30 mL)* butter
1 tbsp. *(15 mL)* cream

Bread Sauce must be made in a double boiler. Put the milk, onion, bay leaf, cloves, salt and pepper in the top of the double boiler and simmer for 20 minutes. (You want the onion to be cooked.) Remove the bay leaf and cloves.

Remove the crusts from the bread and cut the bread into 1" (2.5 cm) cubes.

Add the bread and nutmeg to the sauce, and simmer for 30 to 40 minutes. Remove the sauce from the heat and add the butter and cream; mix thoroughly. Serve hot.

Serves 6 to 8

GRANNY GARRATT *lived to be 96 – with a mind as sharp as a tack. In the last ten years of her life, she could be sitting in a chair, looking as if she might drop dead at any moment, when my Dad would walk in the door and say something to the effect – "London is the ugliest city in the world." or "The Thames is the filthiest river in the world!" or "The English are just a bunch of hired killers!" These words would galvanize her into action and she would give him a proper tongue lashing, leaving her looking 20 years younger and full of life for the rest of the day. Dad would smile; mission accomplished.*

However, when Dad got to the same stage of life himself, I only had to use one word to get him stirred up and bring him back to life, that word was "Trudeau"!

Chicken Paprika

1 large onion, chopped

3 tbsp. *(45 mL)* olive oil
2½-3 lb. *(1.25-1.5 kg)* chicken, cut in
serving-sized pieces

½ tsp. *(2 mL)* salt
1½ tbsp. *(22 mL)* paprika*
2 red or orange peppers
2 large tomatoes

2 cups *(500 mL)* sour cream
2 tbsp. *(30 mL)* flour

Sauté the onion in 1 tbsp. (15 mL) of oil. Set aside.

Fry the chicken in the remaining oil, adding more if necessary. When the chicken is browned, remove the pan from the heat and add the salt, onions and paprika. Return the pan to the heat; cover and simmer for 30 to 35 minutes. If there are not enough natural juices, add a little water. Stir from time to time.

Meanwhile, remove the seeds from the peppers. Slice the peppers into rings. Slice the tomatoes. Set a few pepper rings aside for garnish and put the rest, along with the tomatoes, on top of the chicken. Cover and simmer for 10 minutes.

Combine the sour cream and flour. When the chicken is cooked, pour the sour cream over the chicken and stir into the pan juices. Simmer for only 5 more minutes. Do not let it boil or the sour cream will curdle.

Serve with noodles and a green salad.

Serves 6

* Try this with the real Hungarian paprika to get the best flavour.

This is Eva and Gaspar Molnar's version of a Hungarian classic. Paprikás Csirke (Chicken Paprikash) is traditionally made with chicken browned in bacon fat, but every household has its own recipe. Hungarian paprika is considered the finest type of paprika, other varieties, hot to mild, come from Spain, California and South America.

THE MOLNARS *are Hungarian by birth, Canadian by choice. We met them years ago in Puerto Vallarta. We seem to have a week or two overlap there every year. The talk around the pool is always food and restaurants, unless some European beauty comes to poolside to sunbathe topless. When this happens, the sunglasses go on very quickly, and all conversation ceases.*

Chicken Pot Pie

This family favourite is an on-hand recipe, using some standard pantry ingredients. Chicken Pot Pie is old-fashioned prairie comfort food.

pastry for a single crust, see page 130

¼ cup *(60 mL)* milk
10 oz. *(284 mL)* can cream of chicken soup
¾ cup *(175 mL)* cubed, cooked potato
½ cup *(125 mL)* diced carrots
1½ cups *(375 mL)* diced chicken
½ cup *(125 mL)* frozen peas
10 oz. *(284 mL)* can sliced mushrooms
salt and pepper to taste

Prepare the pastry.

Combine the milk and chicken soup and set aside.

Boil the potatoes and carrots until almost tender. Add the chicken, potatoes and carrots to the milk mixture. Add the peas, mushrooms, salt and pepper.

Place the chicken and vegetables in a deep 10" (25 cm) pie plate or a buttered casserole. Put a lid or foil on the casserole and bake at 350°F (180°C) for 20 minutes, or until the filling is heated through.

With a rolling pin, roll out the pie crust and place it on top of the casserole. Bake at 400°F (200°C) for about 15 minutes, or until the crust is lightly browned.

Serves 4

For oven spills, when something is boiling over in the oven, put a generous amount of either baking soda or salt on the spill. This will stop the spill from burning and possibly catching fire, and make it easier to clean up. If the spill has already caught on fire – dump lots of baking soda on the fire. Been there, done that!!!

Rouladen

rouladen beef steakettes*
 – 1 or 2 per person

Per Rouladen:
mustard
pinch of garlic powder
pinch of salt and pepper
pinch of paprika
cayenne, not too much
half strip of bacon
¼ dill pickle, sliced lengthwise

2, 1 oz. *(34 g)* pkgs. demi-glaze beef
 gravy mix
toothpicks

For each rouladen, lay the steakette flat and spread with mustard. Sprinkle with the spices. Place the bacon at one end, then place the ¼ dill pickle on top of the bacon and roll up. Secure with a toothpick

In a heavy frying pan, brown each beef roll. Place the browned rolls in a casserole or a roaster.

Make the gravy according to the package directions. Spoon the gravy over the rouladen. Cover and bake at 350°F (180°C) for 1¼ to 1½ hours.

Serve the Rouladen with Red Cabbage with Red Wine, Apples, Prunes & Apricots on page 80.

* Rouladen beef steakettes are available at German meat markets or use 4 x 5 x ½" (10 x 13 x 1.3 cm) slices of round steak and pound them with a meat pounder (tenderizer) or kitchen mallet to tenderize and make them a bit thinner.

Quanita Spaeth, a good friend, has a lot of good homestyle German recipes that she has shared with us. This Rouladen is one of our favourites, a simple, tasty shortcut version of a traditional German dish.

If you are making gravy and the roast did not brown the pan enough to give the gravy a nice brown color – put in a teaspoon (5 mL) of instant coffee granules. They work just fine. You can also use wine to deglaze the pan. It gives the gravy a little different flavor – your choice.

If the gravy is too thin, add some more flour; if it is too thick, add more water – pretty basic. BUT – if it is lumpy, get out an electric handheld blender – it can work miracles.

Swiss Steak

Also called smothered, braised or stewed steak in England and the U.S., this is a very versatile and flavourful recipe.

2 lbs. *(1 kg)* round steak ¾-1"
   (2-2.5 cm) thick
¼ cup *(60 mL)* flour
pinch of salt
pinch of pepper
3 tbsp. *(45 mL)* olive oil
1 cup *(250 mL)* chopped celery
1 cup *(250 mL)* chopped onion
2 cups *(500 mL)* sliced mushrooms
2 cups *(500 mL)* canned tomatoes
1 garlic clove, minced
1 tbsp. *(15 mL)* H.P. Steak Sauce

With a kitchen mallet, pound the steak to tenderize and make it thinner.

Cut the steak into serving-sized pieces. Dredge the steak in flour, salt and pepper and fry it until it is brown.

Place the steak in a 2-quart (2 L) casserole or a small roasting pan. Add the celery, onion and mushrooms. Add the tomatoes and juice, minced garlic and H.P. Steak Sauce. Cover and bake at 350°F (180°C) for 1½ hours, or until the meat is tender.

Serves 6

Variations: You may add chili powder; use red wine or beer to replace the tomato liquid; add your favourite herbs: basil, thyme, oregano, sage, rosemary, etc.

DO NOT PUT YOUR GOOD KITCHEN KNIVES in the dishwasher. It dulls them. Wash them in soapy water in the sink and put them away immediately.

If you are ever lucky enough to fall heir to some antique ivory-handled table knives. DO NOT PUT THEM IN THE DISHWASHER – it will ruin the ivory – and make them dull.

Beef Stew

2 lb. *(1 kg)* shoulder or chuck roast
½ cup *(125 mL)* flour
½ tsp. *(2 mL)* salt
½ tsp. *(2 mL)* pepper
½ cup *(125 mL)* olive oil
1 large onion, chopped
1 garlic clove, mashed
4-5 carrots, quartered
4 potatoes, quartered
½ tsp. *(2 mL)* ground savory
½ tsp. *(2 mL)* salt
½ tsp. *(2 mL)* Worcestershire sauce
½ cup *(125 mL)* wine (optional)

2 tbsp. *(30 mL)* flour
½ cup *(125 mL)* water

Cut the roast into 1½" (4 cm) pieces. Roll the meat in the flour, salt and pepper and brown it in the oil.

Place the browned meat in a roasting pan; include the brown crispies from the bottom of the pan.

Sauté the onions and garlic and add to the meat. Cover the meat with water. Cover the roasting pan and bake at 350°F (180°C) for 1½ hours. Check the water level often.

When preparing the vegetables, make sure the carrots are in smaller pieces than the potatoes – so they will cook in the same amount of time. Add the vegetables, savory, salt, Worcestershire sauce and wine to the meat and bake for another 30 minutes.

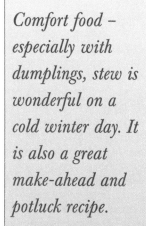

Comfort food – especially with dumplings, stew is wonderful on a cold winter day. It is also a great make-ahead and potluck recipe.

Shake the 2 tbsp. (30 mL) flour with ½ cup (125 mL) water and stir it into the stew to thicken the gravy.

If you are going to have dumplings with the stew, see page 22. Carefully drop the dumplings on top of the hot stew, cover, and return to the oven for 20 to 25 minutes.

Serves 4 to 6

Optional: If you have some Louisiana Roux, page 56, on hand, eliminate the last 2 tbsp. (30 mL) flour and ½ cup (125 mL) of water, and use 2 tbsp. (30 mL) of the Roux.

Savoury Steak

Faye Noble's culinary expertise has improved since her lemon pie experiment recorded below. Her Savoury Steak recipe is hearty, satisfying and delicious.

2 lbs. *(1 kg)* round steak, cut into 1" *(2.5 cm)* cubes
½ cup *(125 mL)* flour
½ tsp. *(2 mL)* salt
½ tsp. *(2 mL)* pepper
2 tbsp. *(30 mL)* olive oil
1 onion, minced
2 tbsp. *(30 mL)* olive oil
1 tsp. *(5 mL)* sugar
½ tsp. *(2 mL)* baking soda
4 cups *(1 L)* canned tomatoes
1 tbsp. *(15 mL)* flour
1 cup *(250 mL)* sour cream
10 oz. *(284 mL)* can sliced mushrooms

Dredge the meat cubes in flour, salt and pepper and brown them in oil in a large frying pan. Set aside.

Sauté the onions in the second 2 tbsp. (30 mL) of oil. Add the meat to the onions in the frying pan and add the sugar, baking soda and the tomatoes. Simmer for 1 hour.

Stir the flour into the cream. Stir into the meat and tomatoes. Add the mushrooms. Heat through and serve with noodles, preferably homemade noodles, see page 82.

Serves 4 to 6

Note: Before you put a jar of tomatoes, or fresh tomatoes into anything with milk in it, for example White Sauce for Tomato Soup, make sure you put some baking soda into the milk solution first. If you do not put the baking soda in first, the white sauce is apt to curdle from the acid in the tomatoes.

FROM *the beginning we knew that Faye was not a "shrinking violet". In fact, she displayed a strength of character envied by all the women in our group. As a newlywed, she spent one day making her husband's favourite pie, lemon. (No pie mixes in those days – it was from scratch.) The lemon pie was proudly displayed in the middle of the kitchen table when he came home from work. Now, there are many things a supportive new husband could have, or should have, said but he chose to say, "What is this s__t?" Faye didn't say a word, she calmly got up, picked up the pie, walked into the bathroom, and flushed it down the toilet. She never, ever, made lemon pie again.*

Hawaiian Beef

2 lbs. *(1 kg)* round steak
2 cups *(500 mL)* red wine
1 cup *(250 mL)* vegetable oil
salt and pepper to taste

1 cup *(250 mL)* carrots cut into ¼"
   (1 cm) pieces
1 cup *(250 mL)* celery, cut into ½"
   (1.3 cm) slices
1 cup *(250 mL)* peppers, cut into ½"
   (1.3 cm) slices
1 cup *(250 mL)* quartered onions
1 cup *(250 mL)* quartered tomatoes
1 cup *(250 mL)* 1" *(2.5 cm)* chopped
   mushrooms

1 tsp. *(5 mL)* Lowry's Seasoning Salt
½ cup *(125 mL)* soy sauce
¾ cup *(175 mL)* brown sugar
4 tbsp. *(60 mL)* olive oil
19 oz. *(540 mL)* can pineapple
   chunks

The night before – cut the steak into 1" (2.5 cm) cubes. Sprinkle the steak with wine, oil, salt and pepper. Stir once or twice and marinate overnight.

Prepare the vegetables the night before and refrigerate them.

Drain the meat, discarding the marinade. In a large, deep frying pan, brown the steak cubes in the oil. Sprinkle with the seasoning salt, add the soy sauce and brown sugar.

Heat the oil in a large frying pan. Add a vegetable to the frying pan every 5 minutes – starting with the carrots and ending with the mushrooms. Keep the pan covered in-between adding the vegetables. Add the pineapple chunks, including the juice, and heat through.

Serves 6

The secret to success with Hawaiian Beef is to simmer it gently and not overcook the vegetables. The fact that you can do so much the night before is a real plus.

If someone spills red wine on the tablecloth, carpet or furniture – use some white wine on it right away. If you don't have white wine – club soda does the trick too.

Baked Chili Beans

This is a recipe from Texas – they use HOT sausage in their chili, if that is what you like, go for it!

1 lb. *(1 kg)* red (kidney) beans
1 garlic clove, minced
2 onions, diced
7½ oz. *(213 mL)* can tomato sauce
2 tsp. *(10 mL)* salt
1 tbsp. *(15 mL)* chili powder
¼ cup *(60 mL)* molasses
1 tsp. *(5 mL)* dry mustard powder
½ cup *(125 mL)* ketchup
2 lbs. *(1 kg)* ground beef OR chorizo sausage meat, sautéed

Wash the beans and place them in a large heavy saucepan. Add water to cover and soak overnight.

In the morning, drain the beans and add all of the remaining ingredients. Add water to cover.

Bake, covered, at 275°F (140°C) for 6 hours. Stir often and add water from time to time, as is necessary.

Serves 8

Sweet Beans & Hamburger

There is a "tease" in every family. My son Mike is ours. He makes this and his kids love it! It's quick and easy when you have run out of ideas.

2 lbs. *(1 kg)* lean ground beef
1 onion, chopped
3 celery stalks, chopped
½ tsp. *(2 mL)* dry mustard powder
salt and pepper to taste
8 oz. *(250 mL)* can tomato sauce
2 cups *(500 mL)* chopped, canned or fresh tomatoes
28 oz. *(796 mL)* can baked beans
½ cup *(125 mL)* brown sugar

In a large heavy saucepan, sauté the ground beef, onion, celery, mustard, salt and pepper until the beef is no longer pink.

Stir in the tomato sauce and tomatoes. Add the beans and sugar. Stir well. Simmer for another 10 minutes. Add a little water, if necessary, to keep it from sticking.

Serves 6

Mexican Goulash

1½ cups *(375 mL)* uncooked
   macaroni

2 lbs. *(1 kg)* ground beef
1 onion, chopped
1 green pepper, chopped
10 oz. *(284 mL)* can sliced
   mushrooms
4 tbsp. *(60 mL)* tomato paste
4 cups *(1 L)* canned tomatoes
½ cup *(125 mL)* chopped pimiento
1 tsp. *(5 mL)* Worcestershire Sauce
1 tsp. *(5 mL)* H. P. Sauce
½ tsp. *(2 mL)* cayenne
salt and pepper to taste

Cook the macaroni and set aside.

In a large frying pan, cook the hamburger, onions, peppers and mushrooms. Add the remaining ingredients.

Last but not least, add the macaroni. Add a little water if additional moisture is needed. Cover and heat through.

Serves 4 to 6

Any time I had to go away, the boys always asked Doug to make Mexican Goulash – the alternative would be a can of beans with a can of sardines. I can understand their preference!

Cornish Pasties

1 recipe of pastry, page 130

Filling Options:
filling for Chicken Pot Pie page 94
   OR
   filling for Tourtière page 107
   OR
   filling for Bereks, page 102

Roll out the pastry dough and cut it in circles about the size of a saucer. Wet the edges of the pastry. Put about a spoonful of filling in the centre of each circle. Fold over and seal the edges, using a fork. Carefully cut small slits in the top of the pastry.

Bake on cookie sheets at 350°F (180°C) for 40 minutes or until nicely browned.

Freeze pasties unbaked. Bake them in the foil when you take them out of the deep freeze, taking the foil off for the last 5 minutes – add 10 minutes to baking time.)

Note: Most kitchen shops have various sizes of Perogy cutters that cut and seal the edges. They range from 3" (8 cm) to 7" (18 cm). The 7" (18 cm) size is perfect for making Cornish Pasties.

Greg, my oldest son, and family organizer, organizes family work/play efforts to make a lot of these. Freeze them in sturdy plastic containers, so they won't get damaged.

Bereks

My mother-in-law, Pauline Martin, and Tilley McCulley were sisters. Working together they would make enough Bereks to feed an army, or so it seemed. The Bereks always disappeared very quickly. Could they have had a phantom at their house, similar to the one at mine, that ate everything that was especially good.

1 recipe of Bun Dough, page 11

Beef and Cabbage Filling:
2 lbs. *(1 kg)* lean ground round
½ head of a small cabbage
2 large onions, finely chopped
4 celery stalks, finely chopped
2 eggs
salt and pepper to taste

Prepare the dough. Let it rise and punch down twice.

Fry the ground beef until it is no longer pink. Add the vegetables and just barely cook them. Set aside to cool. Drain off any moisture.

Add the unbeaten eggs and season to taste.

Now comes the fun part. Roll out the dough to ¼" (1 cm) and cut in 5" (13 cm) squares. The dough will shrink when you cut it, so allow for that.

Put 1 tbsp. (15 mL) of filling in the centre of each square. With a pastry brush, gently brush water around the outside edges of each square. Bring the points to the centre and pinch the edges together, from the outside edges to the centre. Seal well. (If you don't get them sealed you will have juice run out of the buns as they cook.)

Turn the Bereks upside down on cookie sheets and bake at 350°F (180°C) for 15 or 20 minutes, or until they are nicely browned.

Yield: 2 dozen Bereks

Shepherd's Pie

3 cups *(750 mL)* mashed potato

3 cups *(750 mL)* chopped or ground cooked meat – beef, pork, chicken, liver or heart
3 tbsp. *(45 mL)* butter
1 cup *(250 mL)* chopped onion
½ cup *(125 mL)* chopped celery
½ cup *(125 mL)* chopped carrot
1 tbsp. *(15 mL)* flour
½ tsp. *(2 mL)* salt
½ tsp. *(2 mL)* pepper
1 cup *(250 mL)* or more soup stock
½ tsp. *(2 mL)* marjoram
½ tsp. *(2 mL)* dillweed
½ tsp. *(2 mL)* ground oregano
½ tsp. *(2 mL)* ground thyme
1 tsp. *(5 mL)* Worcestershire sauce
1 tsp. *(5 mL)* H.P. Steak Sauce
salt and pepper to taste

If you do not have leftover mashed potatoes, prepare the potatoes.

Cut the meat into small pieces or put it through a grinder.

In a saucepan, melt the butter and sauté the onions, celery and carrots. Stir in the flour, salt and pepper, and add the soup stock. Add the meat. Stir in the spices, Worcestershire sauce, H.P. Steak Sauce, salt and pepper.

Pour the meat mixture into a 2-quart (2 L) buttered shallow casserole. Spread the mashed potatoes on top. Bake at 350°F (180°C) for 45 minutes.

Serves 6

Shepherd's Pie was traditionally the dish that was served on Monday, wash day, to use up the leftovers from Sunday dinner. Wash day was one of those days when housewives were so busy they did not have the time or energy to worry about a lot of food preparation. This hearty dish is satisfying and also portable, great for a potluck or after a hard day on the ski slopes.

If you have oversalted vegetables, try pouring boiling water over them. If they are still too salty, try adding a little cream to them. Sometimes it works – sometimes it doesn't. HOWEVER, if you have oversalted something like a stew – try adding a few more potatoes, and/or other vegetables. Next time be more careful!

Moussaka

Pam Mentis is a good friend as well as a good cook. She is also a sister-in-law to Katina, my daughter-in-law.

6 tbsp. *(90 mL)* olive oil
2 large eggplants, unpeeled, sliced
   1" *(2.5 cm)* thick , coated with
   olive oil and baked

3 cups *(750 mL)* mashed potatoes

Custard:
½ cup *(125 mL)* butter
½ cup *(125 mL)* flour
4 cups *(1 L)* milk
1 tsp. *(5 mL)* salt
pinch EACH of nutmeg and pepper
5 eggs, beaten slightly
¼ cup *(60 mL)* cream

Meat Sauce:
2 lbs. *(1 kg)* ground lean beef
2 onions, finely chopped
2 tsp. *(10 mL)* salt
3 tbsp. *(45 mL)* tomato paste
½ cup *(125 mL)* red wine
3 tbsp. *(45 mL)* chopped parsley
pinch EACH of pepper, cinnamon
   and allspice
2 garlic cloves, minced

1 cup *(250 mL)* grated Parmesan

Oil a 10 x 15 x 2½" (25 x 38 x 6 cm) pan. Prepare the eggplant and bake until soft at 350°F (180°C).

Prepare the mashed potatoes

Custard: Make a **white sauce (béchamel)** by melting the butter, stir in the flour and then the milk, salt, nutmeg and pepper. Cook and stir until thickened. Beat the eggs and cream and stir into the white sauce. Cook and stir until it is smooth and the eggs are cooked. Set aside.

Meat Sauce: Sauté the beef and onions; add the salt, tomato paste and red wine. Stir well. Add the parsley, pepper, cinnamon, allspice and garlic. Set aside.

Arrange the eggplant in the pan. Top with the meat sauce then half of the Parmesan. Top with all of the mashed potatoes, the custard and the remaining Parmesan.

Bake at 350°F (180°C) for 1 hour. Cover with foil for the first ¾ hour, then remove the foil to let the Moussaka brown.

Serves 8

Note: Moussaka originated in Greece but is now popular throughout the Middle East and North America. Ground lamb may be used instead of beef. Sometimes sliced onions or artichokes are included in the layers.

MAIN DISHES – PASTA

Deluxe Lasagne, page 83

Caesar Salad, page 66

Bruschetta, page 43

Tourtière
— French Canadian Meat Pie

pastry for 2 double-crust pies, see
    page 130

1 lb. *(500 g)* ground pork
2 lbs. *(1 kg)* ground veal
1 lb. *(500 g)* ground lamb
1½ cups (375 mL) chopped onion
1 garlic clove, minced
3 large potatoes
1 tsp. (5 mL) salt
1 tsp. (5 mL) ground savory
½ tsp. (2 mL) celery salt
½ tsp. (2 mL) ground cloves
½ tsp. (2 mL) pepper

Sauté the meat until no pink remains. Drain off the fat. Set the meat aside in a large bowl.

Sauté the onions and garlic and add to the meat.

Boil the potatoes and mash well. Combine the potatoes and spices with the meat. Mix well.

With a rolling pin, on a floured work surface, roll out bottom and top crusts for 2, 11" (28 cm) pie plates. Place the bottom crusts in the pie plates.

Spoon the meat filling into the crusts. Brush the rim of the crusts with water and place the top crusts over the filling. Pat the edges with fingers to seal. Cut off the excess pastry and flute the edges. Slash the top crusts to let the steam escape.

Bake at 450°F (230°C) for 10 minutes, then at 350°F (180°C) for 45 minutes, or until done.

Yield: 2 pies; serves 12

Variations: Some recipes add 1½ tsp. (7 mL) of allspice; some add ½ tsp. (2 mL) cinnamon; some add sautéed chopped celery. Sometimes both the meat and potatoes are cut into ½" (1.3 cm) cubes. Many versions of Tourtière do not use potatoes, but the potatoes do add moisture to the texture and a lovely flavour.

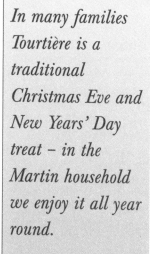

In many families Tourtière is a traditional Christmas Eve and New Years' Day treat – in the Martin household we enjoy it all year round.

Pork Tenderloin in Cranberry Chutney

You know that time is marching on when you get a delicious recipe like this from your granddaughter. This is very easy, very fast and very good, thank you Tracey.

2, 8 oz. *(250 g)* pork tenderloins
3 tbsp. *(45 mL)* olive oil
salt and pepper to taste
⅓ red onion, finely diced
1 cup *(250 mL)* whole-berry
  cranberry sauce
1½ tbsp. *(22 mL)* cider vinegar
1 tsp. *(5 mL)* grated fresh ginger OR
  ½ tsp. *(2 mL)* ground ginger

Slice the pork against the grain into 1" (2.5 cm) thick medallions.

Heat 2 tbsp. (30 mL) of oil in a large non-stick frying pan over medium-high heat.

Salt and pepper both sides of the pork medallions and brown them in the frying pan, just 2 minutes a side, so the outside is brown and the middle is still rare. Remove the pork.

Heat the remaining oil in the pan and add the onion. Cook for 2 minutes, until brown. Add the ginger (if using fresh – cook for 1 minute before adding the other ingredients), the cranberry sauce and the vinegar. Stir until it is combined and just starting to simmer.

Return the pork to the pan. Cover and let simmer for 3 to 4 minutes, until the pork is no longer pink in the centre. Do not overcook or the pork will dry out.

Serves 4

The flavor of ginger will be infused into food quickly if you peel it first. Then put it on a bread board or chopping board and smack it with the flat of a chopping knife or the bottom of a frying pan. This bruises the ginger and allows the flavour to be released more easily.

Very fresh, young, smooth-skinned ginger does not need to be peeled.

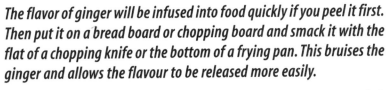

Apple-Pork Stew

2 lbs. *(1 kg)* boneless pork, cut into
   1" *(2.5 cm)* cubes
2 tbsp. *(30 mL)* olive oil
1 cup *(250 mL)* chopped onion
⅓ cup *(75 mL)* flour
pinch of salt
1 tbsp. *(15 mL)* ground thyme
¼ tsp. *(1 mL)* ground sage
1½ cups *(375 mL)* apple juice
1 cup *(250 mL)* chicken broth
1 medium red pepper, sliced
2 cups *(500 mL)* carrots in julienne
   strips
1 cup *(250 mL)* sliced fresh
   mushrooms
12 dried apricot halves
2 large apples, thinly sliced
2 cups *(500 mL)* water

In a large pan, with a good lid, or an electric frying pan, brown the pork cubes in the oil.

Add the onion and cook until translucent. Sprinkle flour over the pork and onions; add salt, thyme and sage. Stir until the flour is absorbed. Gradually stir in apple juice and chicken broth. Bring to a boil, stirring constantly until the sauce is smooth.

Reduce heat to low. Cover and cook for 45 minutes, stirring often. Add water, as needed, to keep the pork from sticking.

When the pork is tender, stir in the peppers, carrots and mushrooms. Cook for 15 minutes. Add apricots and apples and cook for 5 to 10 minutes, until they are tender.

Serve with rice to soak up the juices.

Serves 4 to 6

Pictured on the front cover.

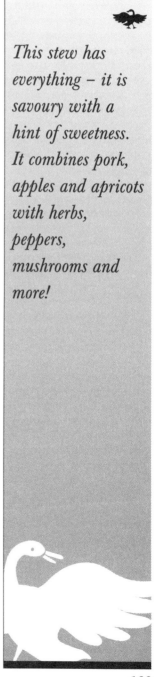

This stew has everything – it is savoury with a hint of sweetness. It combines pork, apples and apricots with herbs, peppers, mushrooms and more!

Jellied Meat Loaf

Great for sandwiches, or with a salad. This recipe of Granny Olsen's is very old and it brings back many memories. When I was growing up it was considered a treat, therefore I must include it. I don't know that any of you dear readers will try it – but I wish you would. You might be pleasantly surprised.

2 pigs' feet
1 large pork hock
2 lbs. *(1 kg)* veal shank
6 peppercorns
1 bay leaf
1 large onion
2 stalks celery
salt and pepper to taste

Put all of the ingredients into a large pot. Cover with cold water and bring to a boil. Remove the foam/scum as it forms. Simmer for 3 to 4 hours, until the meat is very tender.

Discard the bones and skin. Cut the meat into ½" (1.3 cm) pieces and put them in a 4 x 8" (10 x 20 cm) loaf pan. Strain the liquid and skim off any fat. Test the seasoning. Pour the liquid over the meat in the loaf pan. Refrigerate.

As the loaf cools, the fat rises to the surface. Remove the fat before unmoulding the loaf. When you want to serve the meat loaf, turn it out of the pan and slice it. Garnish with parsley sprigs.

Variations: For those that like lamb – 2 lbs. (1 kg) lamb shanks can be substituted for the veal.

Note: Pig's feet (trotters in England or *pieds de porc* in France) are prized in recipes in many countries. The meat is tender, when well cooked, and the flavour is delicious. the hock is the lower part of the hind leg, or the ankle. Both are good sources of natural gelatin.

A bottom layer of sliced hard-boiled eggs, stuffed olives, pickles or gherkins was often added as a decorative accent to Jellied Meat Loaves. Potato salad is a good complement to this dish.

Veal Cutlets Parmigiana

Herbed Garlic Marinade:
2 large garlic cloves, minced
½ tsp. *(2 mL)* dried oregano
1 tbsp. *(15 mL)* minced parsley
1 large onion, thinly sliced
¾ cup *(175 mL)* vegetable oil
1 tbsp. *(15 mL)* lemon juice

2 lbs. *(1 kg)* thin veal cutlets

Coating:
1 cup *(250 mL)* flour
2 eggs, beaten
1 cup *(250 mL)* bread crumbs
½ tsp. *(2 mL)* salt
½ tsp. *(2 mL)* pepper

vegetable oil for frying

Fresh Mushroom Sauce:
3 tbsp. *(45 mL)* butter
3 tbsp. *(45 mL)* flour
1½ cups *(375 mL)* hot milk
½ lb. *(250 g)* mushrooms, sliced

½ cup *(125 mL)* Parmesan cheese

Marinade: Add the garlic, oregano, parsley and onion to the oil and lemon juice. Pour over the veal in a marinating bag or in a shallow dish. If using a dish, cover tightly. Refrigerate for at least 2 hours.

Discard the marinade. Dip the veal cutlets first into the flour, then the beaten eggs, lastly into bread crumbs combined with salt and pepper. Pat to make a firm coating.

Pour ¼" (1 cm) of oil into a frying pan. Heat the oil and sauté a few cutlets at a time. Turn to brown both sides. Place the cutlets in a 9 x 13" (23 x 33 cm) ovenproof pan.

Make a **white sauce** by melting the butter and stirring in the flour until smooth. Add the milk slowly, stirring until smooth. Stir in the mushrooms and heat through.

Spoon the sauce over the veal. Sprinkle with Parmesan and bake at 350°F (180°C) for 40 minutes.

Serves 6

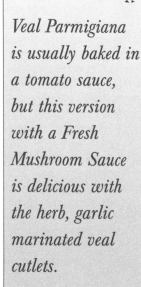

Veal Parmigiana is usually baked in a tomato sauce, but this version with a Fresh Mushroom Sauce is delicious with the herb, garlic marinated veal cutlets.

Note: Cutlets (*scaloppine* in Italian, *escalope* in French) are thin, tender slices of meat that are usually sautéed or grilled quickly.

Dijon Rack of Lamb

Dan is my second son, the perfectionist in the family. When he makes Dijon Rack of Lamb, it not only looks like a picture from a magazine, it is cooked to perfection.

Mustard Coating:
1 garlic clove
½ tsp. *(2 mL)* salt
¼ tsp. *(1 mL)* pepper
¾ tsp. *(3 mL)* crumbled thyme
½ tsp. *(2 mL)* crumbled rosemary
½ tsp. *(2 mL)* paprika
3 tbsp. *(45 mL)* Dijon mustard
4 tbsp. *(60 mL)* olive oil

2 racks of lamb, 1-1¼ lbs.
   (500-625 g) each

¾ cup *(175 mL)* bread crumbs
¼ tsp. *(1 mL)* salt
6 tbsp. *(90 mL)* melted butter,
   divided

Mash the garlic, salt, pepper, thyme, rosemary, paprika, mustard and oil. Paint this mixture over the tops and meaty ends of each rack of lamb.

(This may be prepared several hours ahead of time.) Cover and refrigerate.

Heat oven to 450°F (230°C).

Set the oven rack in the upper middle level. Cover the ends of the ribs with foil. Put the lamb racks in the oven for 12 minutes, then remove.

Combine the bread crumbs, salt and 4 tbsp. (60 mL) of butter. Cover the racks with the crumb mixture. Drizzle 2 tbsp. (30 mL) of butter over the racks.

Turn the oven down to 400°F (200°C) and roast for 15 more minutes.

Serves 2

If you use bread crumbs for frying or baking – it saves time to prepare them ahead. Take the bread crumbs and add the dried herbs that you like; add some Parmesan, some spices. Last but not least, add salt and pepper. Keep the bread crumbs in a container with a good lid, in the refrigerator or freezer.

Desserts
&
Dessert
Sauces

Lemon Snow

Light and refreshing, this is an old-time favourite. Floating Island or Oeufs à la Neige is another very old dessert with mounds of sweetened beaten egg whites poached in simmering milk, which is then used to make the custard.

Lemon Snow:
⅔ cup *(150 mL)* sugar
3 tbsp. *(45 mL)* cornstarch
pinch of salt
1½ cups *(375 mL)* boiling water
3 tbsp. *(45 mL)* fresh lemon juice
2 egg whites, stiffly beaten

Vanilla Custard Sauce:
2 egg yolks
4 tbsp. *(60 mL)* sugar
pinch of salt
1½ cups *(375 mL)* hot milk
1 tsp. *(5 mL)* vanilla

In a large heavy saucepan, combine the sugar, cornstarch and salt. Add boiling water. Cook until thickened and there is no taste of raw starch. Stir constantly to keep from burning. Add the lemon juice. Remove from the heat. Let cool for 20 to 30 minutes, then fold in beaten egg whites. Pour into a bowl or a mould. Chill.

Vanilla Custard Sauce: In the top of a double boiler, beat the egg yolks with a fork; add sugar and salt. Add the hot milk slowly, stirring constantly. Continue simmering until the sauce coats a silver spoon. Remove from the heat and add the vanilla.

Serve the Lemon Snow in stemmed glasses; spoon the Custard over the Snow.

Serves 4

Pictured on page 175.

Lemon Mousse

Tart yet sweet, with the rich flavour of Grand Marnier.

2 tbsp. *(30 mL)* gelatin (2 env.)
4 tbsp. *(60 mL)* water
4 eggs, separated
1½ cups *(375 mL)* sugar
pinch of salt
¾ cup *(175 mL)* fresh lemon juice
⅓ cup *(75 mL)* grated lemon peel
¼ cup *(60 mL)* Grand Marnier
2 cups *(500 mL)* whipping cream

¼ cup *(60 mL)* icing sugar
6 thin lemon slices, halved

Soak the gelatin in the water. In a double boiler, combine the egg yolks, sugar, salt and lemon juice. Cook, stirring constantly, until thickened. Add the lemon peel and simmer until the peel softens. Remove from the heat and add Grand Marnier. Set aside to cool. Whip the cream and fold in the lemon mixture. Pour into a glass bowl or mould. Refrigerate.

Before serving, sprinkle with icing sugar; decorate with lemon slices.

Serves 6

Barbecued Caramel Bananas

Caramel Sauce:
½ cup *(125 mL)* butter
½ cup *(125 mL)* brown sugar
2 tbsp. *(60 mL)* corn syrup
1 cup *(250 mL)* sweetened
  condensed milk

4 green tipped bananas
½ cup *(125 mL)* chopped pecans
  OR walnuts

whipped cream or ice cream
  (optional)

Sauce: Put the butter, sugar, syrup and milk into a heavy saucepan. Heat until boiling. Turn down and continue to simmer for 5 minutes. Stir constantly because this burns very easily. Remove from the heat.

Peel the bananas. Place each banana on a double thickness of foil. Cut the bananas lengthwise or leave whole. Spoon the Caramel Sauce over the bananas. Wrap the bananas, making a double fold on top. Bake at 400°F (200°C) for 10 minutes OR grill over medium heat until hot, about 8 minutes.

Remove the packets from the heat and open carefully. Spoon some of the hot sauce over the bananas. Top with whipped cream or ice cream to make this dish complete.

Serves 4

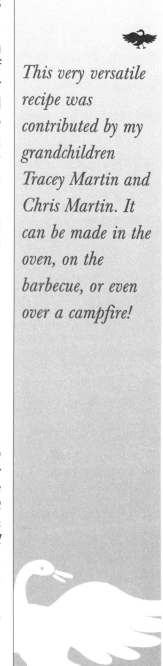

This very versatile recipe was contributed by my grandchildren Tracey Martin and Chris Martin. It can be made in the oven, on the barbecue, or even over a campfire!

TRACEY *was such a funny little girl. From the time she was a baby, she loved the swimming pool. She would reach and gurgle tirelessly to get in, but scream her head off when it was time to get out. No matter how cold it was outside, or how low the temperature of the pool, she wanted in. Early in the spring, the year she was four, she used her great charm on her grandpa to take her out to see if the pool was warm enough. Of course, Grandpa weakened. He took her poolside and held her so she could reach down and dip her little fingers into the icy water. She stood up, eyes shining, and announced, "It's a little bit warm, Grandpa."*

"It's a little bit warm Grandpa," is now a family expression for anything that is darn cold!

Tipsy Crêpes Suzette

Brian's recipe has its own twist – it varies from the classic Crêpes Suzette recipe, which you would expect from such an innovative character – but the important consideration is the flavour, which is wonderful. The original recipe was created by accident, when the liqueurs caught fire, maybe this is an appropriate recipe for Brian.

1 recipe of Crêpes, page 26

Orange Butter Sauce:
½ cup *(125 mL)* butter
¾ cup *(175 mL)* sugar
1 piece lemon rind
2 pieces orange rind
1 cup *(250 mL)* strained orange juice
1 tbsp. *(15 mL)* grated orange rind
2 tbsp. *(30 mL)* Curaçao
2 tbsp. *(30 mL)* Benedictine
¼ cup *(60 mL)* brandy

1 cup *(250 mL)* whipping cream
¼ cup *(60 mL)* sugar
1 tsp. *(5 mL)* vanilla

Prepare the crêpes.

Put the butter and sugar in a heavy pan; heat and stir until the butter darkens a little. Add the lemon and orange rinds, skin side down, and press with a wooden spoon to extract the citrus oils. Add the juice and grated rind. Simmer for a few minutes. Throw out the pieces of rind and stir in the liquors.

Fold the crêpes into quarters and arrange them in a an ovenproof dish; cover with foil. Set the crêpes in a 325°F (160°C) oven and just barely warm them.

To serve, whip the cream until stiff, adding the sugar and vanilla. Pour the sauce over the crêpes and serve with whipped cream.

Serves 8

BRIAN HENDRICKS, *a co-worker, had his masters in practical jokes, along with his university degrees. In the middle of the night before his next door neighbour turned 40, Brian put 40 pink flamingos on the birthday boy's front lawn, with a large Happy Birthday sign. His neighbour looked out in the morning, saw the flamingoes, and had a good chuckle. What he didn't know was that Brian had put a very large sign on his roof, saying "EVERYBODY WELCOME – COME FOR BREAKFAST!" Can you imagine his consternation when the door bell rang nonstop, and neighbours, friends and total strangers started flocking into his house, wishing him happy birthday and looking for breakfast??? Happily, Brian had everything in his own backyard set up to feed any and all comers.*

You can understand why I was skeptical of this recipe, only because it came from Brian. However, the recipe is good, trust me.

Cream Puffs

Choux Paste:
½ cup *(125 mL)* butter
pinch of salt
1 cup *(250 mL)* water
1 cup *(250 mL)* flour
4 eggs

2 cups *(500 mL)* whipping cream,
  whipped
½ cup *(125 mL)* sugar
1 tsp. *(5 mL)* vanilla

chocolate sauce (optional)
strawberries (optional)

Put the butter, salt and water in a small heavy saucepan and bring to a boil. Add the flour all at once and stir like crazy until it forms a ball and the sides of the pan come clean. Remove the dough from the heat and add the eggs 1 at a time. With an electric mixer, beat until smooth between adding each egg.

Drop the dough by spoonfuls onto greased cookie sheets. Bake at 400°F (200°C) for 20 minutes, then reduce to 350°F (180°C) for another 25 minutes. DO NOT OPEN the OVEN until it is time to take the puffs out. Cool on a wire rack.

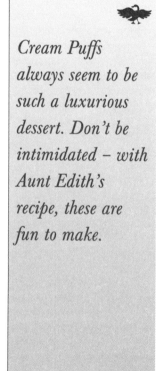

Cream Puffs always seem to be such a luxurious dessert. Don't be intimidated – with Aunt Edith's recipe, these are fun to make.

To serve, prepare the whipped cream, adding the sugar and vanilla. Very close to serving time, cut the tops off the puffs and fill with whipped cream. Pop the tops back on. You may also fill the puffs with the Angel Cake Topping on page 143.

If you want to get really fancy you can drizzle chocolate sauce over the filled Cream Puffs and/or garnish them with strawberries.

Yield: about 16, 3" (8 cm) puffs

Note: Pâte à choux (cream puff paste) can also be used to make eclair shells – just use a pastry bag to form 3 to 4" (7.5 to 10 cm) tubes and bake as for the Cream Puffs. Many Cream Puff recipes add 1 tbsp. (15 mL) sugar for dessert puffs. These puffs don't call for sugar so they may also be used for savoury fillings, e.g., chicken, crab, shrimp or egg salad.

The puffs may also be made bite-sized. These smaller puffs are baked at the higher temperature for 15 to 20 minutes and then at the lower temperature for 10 to 15 minutes.

Note: Some people like to dry out the insides of the puffs by inserting a skewer into the bottom of the baked puffs and inverting them on wire racks to let the steam escape.

Pavlova

Beverley Sharein is the daughter of a friend who moved to Australia over 40 years ago. Her dad, Norm, insists that Bev's Pavlova is the best. (He may be a little prejudiced but certainly this recipe works well for me.)

butter
flour

8 egg whites, room
   temperature
2 tbsp. *(30 mL)* cornstarch
1 tbsp. *(15 mL)* lemon juice
2¾ cups *(675 mL)* icing
   (confectioner's) sugar
1 tsp. *(5 mL)* vanilla

2 cups *(500 mL)* whipping cream
½ cup *(125 mL)* sugar
1 tsp. *(5 mL)* vanilla

fresh strawberries (or any
   other fresh fruit)

Prepare a cookie sheet by lining it with parchment paper. Using a 10" (25 cm) pie plate as a guide, draw 2 circles on the parchment. Lightly butter and flour the circles.

Beat the egg whites slowly; adding the cornstarch and lemon juice as you beat. Increase the speed and beat the whites until they form peaks. Add the sugar 2 tbsp. (30 mL) at a time, beating well between additions. Add the vanilla. Egg whites should be stiff and hold their peaks.

Spread the meringue evenly on the circles and smooth the tops with a wet knife blade. Bake at 200°F (120°C) for 2 hours. Do not open the oven door. Leave the meringues in the oven overnight if you can.

Before serving, whip the cream with the sugar and vanilla until the cream is firm.

Remove 1 meringue from the parchment and place it on a cake platter. Spread with a layer of whipped cream. Place the sliced strawberries on the cream. Place the second meringue on top of the strawberries and cover with the remaining whipped cream. Decorate with strawberries or other fresh fruit.

Serves 10 to 12

Variation: There is a whole world of alternative toppings to strawberries. Lemon Butter, page 131, works well, so does chocolate pudding or pie filling. You can make individual meringues and fill them with fruit sherbet or ice cream and fresh fruit (e.g., blueberries and sliced peaches) — so use your imagination on this one.

Baked Custard/Flan

4 cups *(1 L)* milk
6 eggs
¾ cup *(175 mL)* sugar
pinch of salt
2 tsp. *(10 mL)* vanilla

Scald the milk. Set aside. Beat the eggs slightly; add sugar, salt and vanilla. Gradually add hot milk to the egg mixture – stirring constantly.

Strain (through a sieve or a cloth or both) pour into 8 buttered custard cups, or a 2-quart (2 L) baking dish.

Set the custard cups or baking dish in a pan of hot water, having the water come about halfway up the cups. Bake at 325°F (160°C) for 30 to 35 minutes for small cups, or 40 to 45 minutes for the baking dish, or until a knife inserted in the centre comes out clean. The custard may be served hot or cold.

Serves 6

Variation: To make **Crème Caramel,** place ¾ cup (175 mL) of sugar in a small heavy pan. Drizzle ¼ cup (60 mL) of water over the sugar and heat over medium heat until a clear syrup forms. **Do not stir,** but gently swirl the pan by the handle. Turn heat to high and bring syrup to a boil. Cover and boil for 2 minutes. Uncover and boil until syrup turns a caramel colour. Swirl the pan by the handle and cook until syrup is a dark carmel colour. Quickly pour syrup into unbuttered individual cups or baking dish; swirl to coat bottoms and sides. Let set, then pour in custard and bake as above.

Oh, so simple – but, oh, so good! This Baked Custard is also the base for Crème Caramel.

Apple Crisp

Crumb Mixture:
1 cup *(250 mL)* brown sugar
½ cup *(125 mL)* butter
¾ cup *(175 mL)* flour

6 apples (depending on size), peeled and sliced
1 tsp. *(5 mL)* vanilla OR rum
½ tsp. *(2 mL)* cinnamon OR nutmeg

In a small bowl, cream together the sugar and butter. Rub in the flour until the texture is like coarse crumbs.

Place apple slices into a 2-quart (2 L) buttered casserole. Drizzle with the vanilla; sprinkle with cinnamon.

Sprinkle the crumb mixture over the apples and pat firmly. Bake at 350°F (180°C) for about 40 minutes. Serve with ice cream or whipped cream.

Serves 6

Try rhubarb or peaches and blueberries instead of apples, adding sugar to the filling as needed.

Bread Pudding

This recipe was developed originally to use up the dry ends of bread, in the days when bread was all homemade and had no additives to keep it fresh. The pudding was probably served with real farm cream!

3-4 slices bread 1" *(2.5 cm)* thick
¼ cup *(60 mL)* butter
2 eggs, slightly beaten
½ cup *(125 mL)* brown sugar
2½ cups *(625 mL)* milk
1 tsp. *(5 mL)* vanilla
pinch of salt
½ cup *(125 mL)* raisins (optional)
½ tsp. *(2 mL)* sugar
dash of cinnamon

Remove the bread crusts. Butter the bread slices; cut into cubes and place in a 2-quart buttered casserole.

Combine the eggs, brown sugar, milk, vanilla, salt and raisins, if using. Pour over the bread cubes. Sprinkle with sugar and cinnamon.

Bake at 350°F (180°C) for 45 minutes.

Serves 4

Variation: For a **Saucy Bread Pudding**, serve with Rum Sauce, page 127 or Brown Sugar Sauce, page 127.

Indian Pudding

This dessert by my dear friend Gloria is ideal when you are having a group in for a barbecue.

2 eggs
1 cup *(250 mL)* yellow cornmeal
½ cup *(125 mL)* light molasses
¼ cup *(60 mL)* white sugar
¼ cup *(60 mL)* butter
pinch of salt
¼ tsp. *(1 mL)* baking soda
6 cups *(1.5 L)* hot milk

In a large bowl, beat the eggs, then add cornmeal, molasses, sugar, butter, salt and baking soda. Stir in the hot milk.

Pour into a 4-quart (4 L) buttered roasting pan with a good lid. Bake at 250°F (120°C) for 6 hours. Stir frequently for the first hour, so that the cornmeal does not settle to the bottom.

This should be served with whipped cream or ice cream.

Serves 12

Lemon Sponge Pudding

¾ cup *(175 mL)* sugar
pinch of of salt
¼ cup *(60 mL)* flour
3 tbsp. *(45 mL)* melted butter
1 tsp. *(5 mL)* grated lemon peel
¼ cup *(60 mL)* lemon juice
½ cup *(125 mL)* milk
3 egg yolks, very well-beaten
3 egg whites, stiffly beaten

In a large bowl, combine the sugar, salt and flour. Stir in melted butter, lemon peel and juice. In a separate bowl, combine the milk and egg yolks, then add to the lemon mixture. Fold in the stiffly beaten egg whites.

Pour into an 8" (20 cm) square pan. Set the pudding pan into a larger baking pan. Pour hot water, about 1" (2.5 cm) deep, into the larger pan. Bake at 350°F (180°C) for 40 minutes. Serve hot or cold.

Serves 4 to 6

Beaten egg whites give this pudding a light, airy texture.

Baked Rice Pudding

1 cup *(250 mL)* pearl (short-grain) rice
pinch of salt
1 cup *(250 mL)* sugar
2 tsp. *(10 mL)* vanilla
6 cups *(1.5 L)* milk
½ cup *(125 mL)* raisins (optional)
sprinkle of cinnamon (optional)

Wash the rice and drain well.

Place the rice, salt, sugar, vanilla and milk, plus raisins and cinnamon, if using, into a buttered 2-quart (2 L) casserole.

Bake, covered, at 275°F (130°C) for 3 hours. Stir occasionally. Remove the cover for the last half hour.

Serves 6 to 8

Variation: For ***Lemon Rice Pudding***, omit the cinnamon and add ½ tsp. (2 mL) grated lemon peel and 1 tsp. (15 mL) lemon juice.

For ***Maple Rice Pudding***, use ⅔ cup (150 mL) maple syrup, or more to taste, to replace the sugar. Brown sugar may also be used.

Creamy and comforting, rice pudding is a real treat on a cold winter day. Some people love it with raisins; some do not!

Baked Chocolate Pudding

Hazel McKee's rich chocolate pudding makes its own lovely rich chocolate sauce.

1 cup *(250 mL)* flour
2 tsp. *(10 mL)* baking powder
pinch of salt
¾ cup *(175 mL)* white sugar
2 tbsp. *(30 mL)* cocoa
⅓ cup *(75 mL)* milk
2 tbsp. *(30 mL)* melted butter
1 cup *(250 mL)* chopped nuts

Chocolate Sauce:
1 cup *(250 mL)* brown sugar
4 tbsp. *(60 mL)* cocoa
1¾ cups *(425 mL)* hot water

In a large bowl, combine the flour, baking powder, salt, sugar, cocoa, milk, melted butter and chopped nuts. Beat with an electric mixer until smooth and creamy.

Spread the batter evenly in a buttered 9" (23 cm) square pan.

Sauce: Combine the sugar, cocoa and hot water until smooth and pour over the batter. Bake at 350°F (180°C) for 45 minutes.

Serve hot or cold, with whipped cream or ice cream.

Serves 6

Note: Cocoa beans provide chocolate, cocoa butter and cocoa powder. The cocoa beans grow in pods on *Theobroma cacao* trees which translates to "food of the gods" – very appropriate!

Cocoa powder may be substituted for baking chocolate in an emergency. To substitute for 1 ounce (30 g) of chocolate use 1 tbsp. (15 mL) of butter and 3 tbsp. (45 mL) of cocoa. Dutch cocoa has a higher fat content and a richer flavour.

Tea is also a wonderful product. Soak prunes in tea for additional flavor. Use it to remove fish odors. Leftover tea is great for your houseplants, as well as the compost heap. Use cold tea bags on tired eyes. Soak a cloth in strong tea and use as a compress on sunburns to relieve the pain.

PASTRY & PIES

Rhubarb Sour Cream Pie, page 136

Steamed Pudding

1 cup *(250 mL)* grated carrot
1 cup *(250 mL)* grated potato
1 cup *(250 mL)* sugar
juice of 1 lemon
¼ cup *(60 mL)* marmalade
½ cup *(125 mL)* suet OR butter
2 eggs
1 cup *(250 mL)* flour
½ tsp. *(2 mL)* ground cloves
½ tsp. *(2 mL)* ground nutmeg
½ tsp. *(2 mL)* ground cinnamon
1 tsp. *(5 mL)* baking soda
pinch of salt
1 cup *(250 mL)* raisins, plumped

In a large bowl, combine the carrots, potato, sugar, lemon juice, marmalade, suet and eggs. Stir well.

Add the flour, cloves, nutmeg, cinnamon, baking soda, salt and raisins. Mix thoroughly.

Pour the batter into a buttered 2-quart (2 L) steamed pudding mould. Leave 1" (2.5 cm) headspace for the pudding to expand. Cover the mould with foil, if it doesn't have a lid, and weight it down with a plate. Set the mould on a rack in a larger pan and pour boiling water two-thirds of the way up the side of the mould. Cover the pot and bring to a boil. Reduce the heat to a simmer and steam for 3 hours.

If you do not have steamed pudding moulds, metal coffee cans with metal lids work just as well.

Serve with Brown Sugar Sauce on page 127.

Serves 8 to 10

Note: This type of steamed pudding is English in origin. It is like a moist, soft fruit cake. A flaming Plum Pudding was a much-loved Christmas tradition. However, the old English word for "raisin" was "plum", so you are not likely to find many recipes actually using plums!

MY GRANDMOTHERS *both made wonderful steamed puddings on a regular basis. They used carrot or potato or apple, whichever needed to be used up the quickest. The only time they put raisins in the pudding was at Christmas time. They actually steamed their puddings in cleaned, bleached, scrubbed, ten-pound sugar sacks. Don't ask me why the pudding didn't get soggy – but it didn't.*

Granny Garratt's Steamed Pudding is moist and has a delicious combination of spices. If you can't find suet, don't worry, butter is a good substitute.

Ginger Yogurt Sauce

This tangy sauce enhances whatever fresh fruit is in season.

2 cups *(500 mL)* firm plain yogurt
½ cup *(125 mL)* ginger marmalade
½ cup *(125 mL)* brown sugar
2 tsp. *(10 mL)* fresh lemon OR lime juice

Combine all of the ingredients in a bowl. Cover and refrigerate so that the flavours mellow.

This sauce can be spooned over fresh fruit or served in small cups as a light dessert.

Yield: about 2½ cups (625 mL) of sauce

Blueberry Sauce

This sauce is great on angel food cake or ice cream. In fact, it is also very good on waffles.

2 cups *(500 mL)* crabapple, grape or your favourite jelly
5 tbsp. *(75 mL)* water
5 tbsp. *(75 mL)* honey
5 tbsp. *(75 mL)* lemon juice
½ tsp. *(2 mL)* cinnamon
½ tsp. *(2 mL)* nutmeg
5 tbsp. *(75 mL)* rice flour
9 cups *(2.25 L)* blueberries

Combine all of the ingredients, except the blueberries, in a large saucepan. Simmer for 5 minutes then stir in the berries. Continue simmering only until the berries are heated through.

Serve hot.

Store in the refrigerator for up to 2 days, or put any leftover sauce in resealable freezer bags and freeze until needed. Reheat before serving.

Yield: about 2 quarts (2 L) of sauce

Rum Sauce

1½ cups *(375 mL)* sugar
1½ cups *(375 mL)* corn syrup
½ cup *(125 mL)* butter
2 cups *(500 mL)* light cream OR
   coffee cream
½ tsp. *(2 mL)* vanilla
3 tbsp. *(45 mL)* light rum

In a heavy saucepan, combine the sugar, syrup, butter and 1 cup of cream. Bring to the boiling point and cook to the firm ball stage or 244°F (120°C).

Add the remaining cream and lower the heat. Cook for 15 minutes more. Cool for a few minutes, then add the vanilla and rum.

Store any leftover sauce in a covered container in the refrigerator. This sauce may be served warm or cold.

Yield: about 4 cups (1 L) of sauce

Warm Rum Sauce on fresh Apple Pie or Bread Pudding – it's wonderful!

Brown Sugar Sauce

1 cup *(250 mL)* brown sugar
3 tbsp. *(45 mL)* flour
2 cups *(500 mL)* boiling water
2 tbsp. *(30 mL)* butter
1 tsp. *(5 mL)* vanilla

In a heavy saucepan, combine the sugar, flour and boiling water. Bring to the boiling point, stirring constantly until thickened. Simmer until the flour is cooked.

Remove the sauce from the heat and stir in the butter and vanilla.

Store any leftover sauce in a covered container in the refrigerator. Reheat before serving.

Yield: about 2 cups (500 mL) of sauce

Note: Use this sauce on steamed puddings as well as plain puddings or cakes. It is also very good on ice cream.

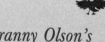

Granny Olson's Brown Sugar Sauce is the most versatile, useful sauce recipe you will ever find. It is not terribly sweet, but very tasty.

Double Chocolate Sauce

You will be tasting this as you go along! It is great on ice cream!

6 oz. *(170 g)* butter
6 oz. *(170 g)* dark chocolate
¾ cup *(175 mL)* sugar
¾ cup *(175 mL)* cocoa
1 tsp. *(5 mL)* instant coffee
½ tsp. *(2 mL)* cinnamon
½ cup *(125 mL)* corn syrup
1¼ cups *(310 mL)* whipping cream
1 tsp. *(5 mL)* vanilla

In a heavy saucepan, melt the butter and chocolate. Add the sugar, cocoa, coffee, cinnamon, corn syrup and whipping cream. Bring to the boiling point; stir and simmer until the sugar has dissolved. Continue to simmer until the consistency thickens just a little.

Remove the pan from the heat and stir in the vanilla.

Store any leftover sauce in a covered container in the refrigerator. This sauce may be served warm or cold.

Yield: about 4 cups (1 L) of sauce

Peanut Butter Sauce

This sauce is delicious with a chocolate or spice cake as well as with ice cream.

1 cup *(250 mL)* peanut butter, smooth or chunky
1 cup *(250 mL)* corn syrup or honey
2 tbsp. *(30 mL)* hot water

Put all of the ingredients into a heavy saucepan. Heat it just enough for the sauce to become smooth. Stir constantly.

Serve over ice cream and bananas or just ice cream.

Store any leftover sauce in a covered container in the refrigerator. Reheat before serving.

Yield: about 2 cups (500 mL) of sauce

Note: Try this sauce with chocolate ice cream – however I don't want to hear that you are eating the sauce by the spoonful!

Pastry & Pies

Pie Pastry

Lou Garratt, my dad, always made the best pies. This is his pastry recipe.

5 cups *(1.25 L)* flour
1 tsp. *(5 mL)* salt
1 tbsp. *(15 mL)* sugar
1 lb. *(454 g)* Tenderflake lard, chilled
2 tbsp. *(30 mL)* chilled butter
1 cup *(250 mL)* ice water

Sift the flour, salt and sugar into a large bowl or food processor.

Cut in the lard and butter or place it in the food processor and use an on/off motion until the particles are the the size of small peas or cornmeal.

Drizzle with just enough water to make the pastry form a ball. Refrigerate until you are ready to use.

Roll out the pastry, with a rolling pin, on a floured canvas or pastry board.

Caution: do not overwork pie pastry – too much handling toughens the dough.

Yield: 4 double pie crusts/8 single pie crusts

Divide any leftover pastry into pie-sized portions and freeze in resealable freezer bags.

DAD'S *cooking was simple, plain, everyday food. For him, happiness was to be in the kitchen. He had a lot of requests for his apple pies and his lemon pies. He loved making both of them if he was expecting company. Dad was very quick to share most of his recipes with anyone that asked – except the lemon pie recipe – which he kept as close to his chest as a poker player does his cards. People always raved – "Lou's lemon pie is the best we have ever eaten." Dad would smile from ear to ear as he generously passed around seconds – but not the recipe. It was a shock when he finally divulged his great secret – he used Jell-o Lemon Pie Filling for the filling and three egg whites for the meringue on top! (It's not surprising he never had a failure – perfection every time!)*

Butter Tarts

pie pastry, page 130

4 tbsp. *(60 mL)* butter
3 cups *(750 mL)* brown sugar
3 eggs
1 tsp. *(5 mL)* vinegar
2 tsp. *(10 mL)* vanilla
2 tbsp. *(30 mL)* flour
1 cup *(250 mL)* currants OR raisins
½ cup *(125 mL)* walnuts or pecans

With a rolling pin, on a floured surface, roll out the pastry and place the tart shells very gently into muffin tins.

Mix together the butter, sugar and eggs. Stir in the vinegar and vanilla, then the flour, currants and nuts.

The secret to having success is making the tart shells large enough to come to the top of the muffin tins, and being careful not to use too much filling. Spoon 1 tsp. (5 mL) of filling into each tart shell. Bake at 350°F (180°C) for 15 to 20 minutes. You must watch them carefully.

Everybody in the world loves butter tarts – Monas Helm made the best! Butter Tarts are a Canadian specialty and recipes vary from region to region.

Yield: 5 dozen, 2³/₄" (7 cm) tarts

If there is a little dough left over, bake empty tart shells to put in the deep freeze for the Lemon Butter tarts below.

Lemon Butter

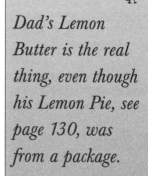

½ lb. *(227 g)* butter
5 lemons, grated rind and juice of
4 cups *(1 L)* sugar
12 eggs, well beaten

In a double boiler, over simmering water, melt the butter. Add lemon rind and cook for a few minutes, until softened. When rind has softened, add the juice, sugar and eggs; stir often. Cook until it is the consistency of honey, about 20 minutes.

Dad's Lemon Butter is the real thing, even though his Lemon Pie, see page 130, was from a package.

Dad processed his Lemon Butter in jars but it is best to put it in small resealable freezer bags and freeze it. It keeps its colour and thaws quickly. Lemon Butter (or Curd) keeps, refrigerated, for about 1 week.

P.S. Keep the baked tart shells in the freezer also.

Yield: about 4 cups (1 L) of Lemon Butter

IN DAYS *gone by, people simply dropped in if they were nearby. Our household was ever on the ready for unexpected company. Dad always had this prepared before the Holiday Season. We also had prepared tart shells – put a spoonful of lemon butter in a tart shell, add a dollop of whipped cream and Voila!! A delightful treat.*

Duff's Miracle Meringue

1 tbsp. *(15 mL)* cornstarch
2 tbsp. *(30 mL)* cold water
½ cup *(125 mL)* boiling water

3 egg whites
pinch of salt
6 tbsp. *(90 mL)* sugar
1 tsp. *(5 mL)* vanilla

Duffy Martin, made the best meringue, it was always perfect. This meringue cuts beautifully and does not get sticky. It takes a little more time to make, but it is well worth it.

Blend the cornstarch and cold water in a saucepan. Add the boiling water and cook, stirring constantly, until clear and thickened. Let stand until completely cold.

With an electric beater, at high speed, beat the egg whites and salt until peaks form. Gradually add the sugar and beat until stiff. Turn the mixer to low speed and add the cold cornstarch mixture. Mix thoroughly.

Spread the meringue over the cooled pie filling, making sure you get right to all of the edges of the pastry to seal it completely. Bake at 350°F (180°C) for 12 minutes, or until slightly browned.

Yield: meringue for 1 pie

DUFFY MARTIN *was a distant cousin. Over the years I questioned her as to how she made such a wonderful meringue. Her reply was always the same – she put cornstarch in it. What she didn't tell me, until just before her passing, is that you must cook the cornstarch and cool it. This is one of those recipes that you don't ever want to lose!*

Key Lime Chiffon Pie

baked 9" (23 cm) single-crust pastry shell, see page 130

1¼ cups *(310 mL)* sugar
2 egg yolks, slightly beaten
pinch of salt
½ cup *(125 mL)* fresh lime juice
1 tsp. *(5 mL)* grated lime rind
1 tbsp. *(15 mL)* gelatin
½ cup *(125 mL)* cold water
4 drops green food colouring
2 egg whites, stiffly beaten
1 cup *(250 mL)* whipping cream, whipped

lime slices for garnish

Prepare the pie shell.

Combine 1 cup (250 mL) of sugar, the egg yolks, salt, ¼ cup (60 mL) lime juice and grated rind in the top of a double boiler. Cook over simmering water until thick.

Soften the gelatin in the cold water and add to the thickened lime mixture. Cool.

Stir in the rest of the juice and the colouring. Cool the filling until it starts to set.

Beat the egg whites with the remaining sugar. Fold into the filling. Whip the cream and fold in.

Pour the filling into the shell and refrigerate for 4 to 6 hours or overnight. Garnish with lime slices. Keep refrigerated until just before serving.

Serves 6

Variation: To make **Lemon Chiffon Pie**, substitute ½ cup (125 mL) fresh lemon juice and 1 tsp. (5 mL) grated lemon rind for the lime juice and rind.

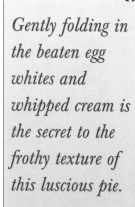

Gently folding in the beaten egg whites and whipped cream is the secret to the frothy texture of this luscious pie.

Handle pie dough gently. Do not overwork it or you will toughen it. (Gluten-free flour is especially delicate. Use parchment paper in rolling it out. Gluten-free flour is: 2 cups (500 mL) rice flour, ⅔ cup (150 mL) potato flour and ⅓ cup (75 mL) tapioca flour.

Flapper Pie

Flapper Pie is a western Canadian version of cream pie, with a graham-wafer crumb crust. It was a great prairie favourite in the 1920s and it deserves to become a favourite again.

Brown Sugar Crumb Crust:
1½ cups *(375 mL)* graham wafer crumbs
⅓ cup *(75 mL)* brown sugar
½ cup *(125 mL)* melted butter
½ tsp. *(2 mL)* cinnamon

Flapper Pie Filling:
¾ cup *(175 mL)* sugar
3 tbsp. *(45 mL)* cornstarch
3 egg yolks, slightly beaten
2 cups *(500 mL)* milk
1 tsp. *(5 mL)* vanilla
1 tbsp. *(15 mL)* butter

Meringue:
3 egg whites
6 tbsp. *(90 mL)* sugar
1 tsp. *(5 mL)* vanilla

Crust: Combine all of the crust ingredients and set aside ¼ cup (60 mL) of crumbs for the topping. Press the remaining crumbs into an 11" (28 cm) pie plate. Bake at 350°F (180°C) for 8 minutes. Cool.

Filling: Combine the sugar and cornstarch in a heavy saucepan (not aluminum). Add the egg yolks to the milk and pour them over the sugar and cornstarch. Stir constantly over medium heat until the filling thickens. Cool.

Just before serving, pour the filling into the shell.

Meringue: Beat the egg whites until stiff, adding the sugar gradually. Add the vanilla. Spread the meringue to all of the edges of the crust. Sprinkle the remaining crumbs on top.

Bake at 350°F (180°C) for 12 minutes, until just beginning to brown.

Serves 6

Variations: For **Banana Cream Pie**, arrange banana slices in the baked pie shell. Top with the Flapper Pie filling and then the meringue. Bake as above.

For **Coconut Cream Pie**, add 1 cup (250 mL) of flaked coconut to the Flapper Pie filling and proceed as above.

When you are going to bake a frozen pie, before putting it in the oven, cut a circle about the size of a dollar coin from the centre of a piece of foil. Snip 6 cuts, 2" (5 cm) long, from the centre toward the edge before you put it on the pie. Place the foil on the pie. Bake at 400-410°F (200-205°C) for about 1 hour. Take the foil off for the last 5 to 10 minutes to brown the crust.

Pumpkin Pie

pastry for a single-crust 9" (23 cm)
   pie, see page 130

Pumpkin Pie Filling:
⅔ cup *(150 mL)* brown sugar
½ tsp. *(2 mL)* cinnamon
½ tsp. *(2 mL)* ginger
½ tsp. *(2 mL)* salt
1¼ cups *(310 mL)* pumpkin, canned
   or cooked
2 eggs, slightly beaten
1 cup *(250 mL)* evaporated milk
⅓ cup *(75 mL)* orange juice

1 cup *(250 mL)* whipping cream
3 tbsp. *(45 mL)* sugar
1 tsp. *(5 mL)* vanilla

Prepare the pie crust.

In a large bowl, combine all of the filling ingredients, mixing well. Pour into the unbaked shell.

Bake at 450°F (230°C) for 10 minutes then reduce to 325°F (160°C) for 45 minutes. Cool.

Whip the cream until thickened. Gradually add the sugar and vanilla, beating until the cream holds stiff peaks.

Just before serving, spread the whipped cream over the pie, or serve the cream on the side.

Serves 6

This Pumpkin Pie is too good to serve only at Thanksgiving. With canned pumpkin we can make it at anytime.

Apple Pie

pastry for a double-crust 11"
   (28 cm) pie, see page 130

2 tbsp. *(30 mL)* butter
1 cup *(250 mL)* sugar
2 tbsp. *(30 mL)* flour
5-6 apples sliced
sprinkle of cinnamon OR nutmeg

Glaze: (optional)
1 egg, beaten with a little milk
sprinkle of sugar

Roll out the pastry and place it in the pie plate. Rub butter over the bottom crust. Combine the sugar and flour. Sprinkle 1 tbsp. (15 mL) of the sugar/flour mixture over the bottom crust. Arrange the apple slices in the bottom shell, adding the sugar mixture as you go. Dab the remaining butter on top of the apples and sprinkle with cinnamon.

Brush water on the edge of the bottom crust. Place the top crust in place, cut off excess crust; seal and flute the edges; cut steam vents.

To make Dad's Apple Pie an extraordinary finale to a meal, serve it with Hot Rum Sauce on page 127.

If you wish, brush the top crust with egg beaten with milk, then sprinkle with sugar. Bake at 400°F (200°C) for 15 minutes, lower the heat to 350°F (180°C) for 30 minutes.

Serves 6 to 8

Rhubarb Sour Cream Pie

Aunt Edith's Rhubarb Sour Cream Pie has become the favourite pie at our house.

pastry for a double-crust 11"
   (28 cm) pie, see page 130

3 cups *(750 mL)* finely chopped red
   rhubarb
1 cup *(250 mL)* sugar
1 tbsp. *(30 mL)* flour
1 cup *(250 mL)* sour cream
2 eggs, slightly beaten
pinch of salt
1 tsp. *(5 mL)* almond OR vanilla
   extract

Glaze: (optional)
1 egg, beaten with a little milk
sprinkle of sugar

Prepare the pastry.

Wash the rhubarb and cut it into ¼" (1 cm) pieces.

Combine the sugar and flour. Add the sour cream, eggs, salt and flavouring. Add the rhubarb and mix thoroughly.

Pour the rhubarb into the bottom crust. Brush the edges of the crust with water. Place the top crust in place and cut off the excess; seal and flute the edges; cut steam vents. Brush the top crust with the egg mixture and sprinkle with sugar.

Bake at 400°F (200°C) for 10 minutes then lower the heat to 350°F (180°C) for about 40 minutes, or until the crust is a light brown.

Serves 8

Pictured on page 123.

EDITH, *had a real zest for living. Cooking and gardening were not her only interests. She loved fishing, handicrafts, canasta, dancing, cats, dogs, kids and curling – life in general.*

The only thing she truly disliked was ironing. With the arrival of her first deep freeze she developed the habit of rolling up the damp ironing and putting it in a 50-pound sugar sack in the deep freeze – to be brought out the minute I walked in the door. As it thawed, it was perfect for ironing.

Helping people was second nature to my dear aunt. If you had walked though her door on any given day and said, "I'm going to have to whip the world." She would have calmly started rolling up her sleeves and said, "Where should we start?"

Edith had a great influence on my life. It was wonderful, growing up as an only child, knowing that I could always count on her to be on my team!

Saskatoon Pie

pastry for a double-crust 11"
 (28 cm) pie, see page 130

4 cups saskatoons
½ cup *(125 mL)* water
2 tbsp. *(30 mL)* lemon juice
pinch of salt

1 cup *(250 mL)* sugar
1 tbsp. *(15 mL)* flour
1 tsp. *(5 mL)* grated lemon rind

Glaze:
1 egg beaten with a little milk
sprinkle of sugar

Prepare the pastry.

Wash the berries and place them in a large heavy saucepan. Add the water, lemon juice and salt; bring to a boil and simmer until the water is almost gone. Cool.

Combine the sugar, flour and lemon rind and stir into the cooled berries.

Pour the filling into the bottom crust. Brush the edges of the crust with water. Put the top crust in place. Cut off the excess crust; seal and flute the edges; cut steam vents. Brush the top crust with the beaten egg mixture and sprinkle with sugar.

Bake at 400°F (200°C) for 10 minutes, then lower the heat to 350°F (180°C) for 40 minutes, until the crust is light brown.

Serves 8

W HEN I *was a kid – berry picking (saskatoons) generally happened near the end of July or the first of August. My granny spent the day before preparing the picnic lunch, and early on Sunday morning we all piled into the truck, some in the front, most in the back, and off we went. Aunts, uncles and neighbours met us at a designated, predetermined berry patch. We each had our own Rogers Golden Syrup pail with a handle. The adults hung their pails from their belts and filled them in no time at all! I had to struggle all day to get my little pail half full! (Either I ate too many, or the bushes were too tall – I don't know which.)*

Lunch always seemed like a banquet (remember there were no paper plates or cups in those days – everyday dishes were brought along and had to be washed upon our return home.) The cold Watkins Orangeade and Lemonade were a special treat – kept cold by the jug being set into a hole dug on the shady side of a tree or bush. By four o'clock everyone headed home to do the evening chores, tired – but happy!

Saskatoons have a distinctive tart flavour that is wonderful in pies, jams and jellies. First Nations people across the prairies used them in pemmican, soups and stews. In the U.S. they are known as serviceberries, June berries or shadberries.

137

O-So-Good Raisin Pie

*Raisin Pie is a
favourite at
Prairie Fowl (or
Fall) Suppers.
Aunt Hazel
Olsen's recipe is a
family treasure.*

baked 9" (23 cm) single-crust pastry
    shell, see page 130

Raisin Filling:
1 cup *(250 mL)* sugar
1 tbsp. *(15 mL)* flour
3 egg yolks
2 tsp. *(10 mL)* vinegar
½ tsp. *(2 mL)* cinnamon
½ tsp. *(2 mL)* nutmeg
½ tsp. *(2 mL)* cloves
1 cup *(250 mL)* yellow raisins,
    plumped
1 cup *(250 mL)* boiling water

Meringue;
3 egg whites
6 tbsp. *(90 mL)* sugar
1 tsp. *(5 mL)* vanilla

Prepare the pastry shell.

For the filling, combine the sugar,
flour, yolks, vinegar, spices and
raisins in a heavy saucepan. Add
the boiling water and cook gently
until the filling thickens. Pour into
the baked pie shell.

Meringue: Beat the egg whites
with an electric mixer, gradually
adding the sugar, until stiff peaks
form and sugar is dissolved. Add
the vanilla.

Spread the meringue over the pie
filling, spreading it to all of the
edges of the pastry to seal.

Bake at 350°F (180°C) for 12 minutes, or until meringue browns
slightly.

Serves 6

Variations: You could soak the raisins in a bit of rum. (My idea – not Aunt
Hazel's – don't tell her!)

AUNT HAZEL *is a dear old soul. In her 89th year, she is still living
on the family farm in southern Saskatchewan. She is also still serving
homemade cookies when you stop by for coffee!!*

Cakes
&
Squares

Coffee Cheesecake

My daughter-in-law Katina is a great source of gourmet desserts. She hit the jackpot with this one! It's a winner.

Oreo Cookie Crust:

1½ cups *(375 mL)* Oreo cookie crumbs

½ cup *(125 mL)* melted butter

3 tbsp. *(45 mL)* sugar

Espresso Filling:

3, 8 oz. *(250 g)* pkgs. cream cheese

1 cup *(250 mL)* sugar

2 tsp. *(10 mL)* vanilla

4 eggs

½ cup + 2 tbsp. *(155 mL)* flour

3 tbsp. *(45 mL)* cold espresso

Sour Cream Topping:

1⅓ cups *(325 mL)* sour cream

3 tbsp. *(45 mL)* sugar

1 tsp. *(5 mL)* vanilla

1 tbsp. *(15 mL)* cold espresso

¾ cup *(175 mL)* whipping cream, whipped

2 oz. *(50 g)* chocolate, shaved

24 chocolate coffee beans

Crust: Combine the crumbs, butter and sugar and press into a 12" (30 cm) cheesecake pan lined with foil. Bake at 350°F (180°C) for 10 minutes.

Filling: In a large bowl, beat together the cream cheese, sugar and vanilla. Add the eggs, 1 at a time, and beat well after each addition. Add ⅓ of the flour at a time, and beat well after each addition. Beat in the coffee. Pour the filling over the crumb mixture and bake for 25 to 35 minutes. The cheesecake will be a little soft in the middle – do not over bake.

Topping: Combine the sour cream, sugar, vanilla and espresso. Pour the topping over the cheesecake and return to the oven for 10 minutes.

Cool the cheesecake and refrigerate until ready to serve. Just before serving, decorate with whipped cream, shaved chocolate and chocolate coffee beans.

Serves 10 to 12

Pictured opposite.

If you need sour milk and you don't have it – just add a few drops of lemon juice or vinegar to whole milk. Let it sit a minute and give it a quick stir. If you need 1 cup (250 mL) of sour cream, you can substitute ¾ cup (175 mL) of milk, ¾ tsp. (3 mL) lemon juice and ⅓ cup (75 mL) butter.

CAKES

Coffee Cheesecake, page 140

Angel Food Cake

1¼ cups *(310 mL)* flour
1½ cups *(375 mL)* sugar
12 egg whites
¼ tsp. *(1 mL)* salt
1 tsp. *(5 mL)* cream of tartar
1 tsp. *(5 mL)* vanilla
1 tsp. *(5 mL)* almond flavouring

Chocolate Variation: Omit vanilla
and almond and add:
½ cup *(125 mL)* cocoa
½ cup *(125 mL)* warm water

Espresso Variation: Omit vanilla
and almond and add:
1 tbsp. *(15 mL)* instant coffee
    granules
2 tsp. *(10 mL)* grated lemon peel

Sift the flour and sugar together and set aside.

With an electric mixer, beat the egg whites, salt and cream of tartar until STIFF but not dry. (If it can hold a tablespoon upright – it is just right.) Add the flavourings. Gently fold in the flour/sugar mixture 2 tbsp. (30 mL) at a time. Fold, do not beat. Stir only until the flour is mixed in. Pour the batter into an angel food pan (10 x 4" [25 x 10 cm] tube pan).

Bake at 325°F (160°C) for 60 minutes. Invert the pan over the neck of a bottle to cool, about 2 hours.

Serves 10 to 12

Aunt Edith made the lightest, fluffiest Angel Food Cakes. I love the ads that say that there is NO FAT in Angel Food Cake. Can we take that to mean that Angel Food Cake is a health food?

WE USED *to beat the egg whites with a rotary beater. They had to be stiff enough to hold a silver tablespoon upright – you had to rest your arms a bit in the process or take turns. Now it takes a few minutes with a good electric mixer.*

Angel Cake Topping

1 tbsp. *(15 mL)* gelatin (1 env.)
¼ cup *(60 mL)* water
3 eggs, separated
1 cup *(250 mL)* sugar
⅓ cup *(75 mL)* orange juice
⅓ cup *(75 mL)* lemon juice
1 cup *(250 mL)* whipping cream

Soften the gelatin in the water.

In the top of a double boiler over simmering water, beat the egg yolks. Add the sugar and juices and cook until thick. Add the softened gelatin. Set aside and cool.

Whip the egg whites until stiff and fold into the cooled thickened sauce.

Whip the cream until stiff and fold into the cooled sauce. Spread on the top and sides of the cake.

Sufficient for 1 large Angel Food Cake

This is a deluxe creamy citrus-flavoured topping.

Sunshine Cake

This recipe is as old as your great grandmother, and just may have been her favourite.

12 egg yolks
1½ cups *(375 mL)* sugar
¾ cup *(175 mL)* warm water
4 tbsp. *(60 mL)* lemon juice
¼ tsp. *(1 mL)* salt
1 tbsp. *(15 mL)* grated lemon rind
2 cups *(500 mL)* flour
4 tsp. *(20 mL)* baking powder

In a large bowl, with an electric mixer, beat the egg yolks until thick and creamy. Slowly add the sugar and continue beating. Add the remaining liquids and dry ingredients alternately. Beat slowly until everything is thoroughly mixed.

Pour the batter into a 10 x 4" (25 x 10 cm) tube pan and bake at 325°F (160°C) for 60 minutes.

Cool and frost with Boiled Frosting, see below.

Serves 10 to 12

Note: If you have made Meringues and don't quite have 12 yolks, measure the yolks you do have in a measuring cup and top them up to 1 cup (250 mL) with water. You do need to have at least 8 yolks.

THIS *recipe was originally developed to use up the yolks left over from Angel Food Cakes. In those days absolutely nothing went to waste – especially yolks from 12 precious eggs!! Both cakes were usually made the same day, because there was no refrigeration.*

Boiled Frosting

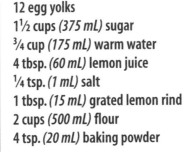

Similar to the well-known Seven-Minute Frosting, I think this frosting is even better – it is also fat free!

½ cup *(125 mL)* water
1½ cups *(375 mL)* sugar
2 tbsp. *(30 mL)* corn syrup
3 egg whites
pinch of cream of tartar
pinch of salt
1 tsp. *(5 mL)* vanilla

Combine the water, sugar and syrup in a heavy saucepan. Cover and bring slowly to a boil. (Cover the pan to keep the sugar from crystallizing on the edges.) Once it is almost to a boil, uncover and bring to the soft ball stage, 238°F (115°C).

Beat the egg whites, cream of tartar, salt and vanilla until stiff. Continue beating and pour the hot syrup slowly into the egg whites. Beat until very glossy, until the frosting stands up in peaks.

Yield: sufficient for a large layer cake or bundt or tube cake.

Lemon Chiffon Cake

2 cups *(500 mL)* sifted flour
1½ cups *(375 mL)* sugar
3 tsp. *(15 mL)* baking powder
pinch of salt
½ cup *(125 mL)* vegetable oil
7 egg yolks
¾ cup *(175 mL)* cold water
1 lemon, juice of
1 tsp. *(5 mL)* grated lemon rind
1 cup *(250 mL)* egg whites
½ tsp. *(2 mL)* cream of tartar

Sift the dry ingredients into a large bowl. Make a well in the dry ingredients and pour in the oil, egg yolks, water, lemon juice and rind. Mix thoroughly with an electric mixer.

Beat the egg whites and cream of tartar with an electric mixer until stiff. Fold the batter gently into the egg whites.

Pour into an ungreased 10 x 4" (25 x 10 cm) tube pan.

Bake at 325°F (160°C) for 60 minutes, or until the cake springs back when touched.

Serves 10 to 12

Variations: For **Orange Chiffon Cake**, substitute an equal amount of orange juice for the water, and grated orange rind for the lemon rind.

Peggy Lawson's Lemon Chiffon Cake is fluffy, moist and tender. The oil replaces butter or shortening, so chiffon cakes do not dry out as readily as do other cakes. They also freeze well, so they can be sliced into layers and filled with your favourite flavours of ice cream or frozen yogurt. Refreeze filled cakes overnight or for 3 to 4 hours before serving.

PEG, *a dear friend, was one of those delightful people who spoiled everyone and everything around her, including a squirrel in her backyard. She felt that her squirrel really preferred pistachio nuts over any other kind. Jake, her husband, who was never at a loss for words, had a lot to say about the squirrel and its diet. However, Peg did not back down. She continued feeding her squirrel with the rich diet of pistachios until it eventually mysteriously disappeared. As you can well imagine, there were a lot of theories about its demise.*

White Layer Cake

A good basic white cake recipe is to be treasured. Aunt Tilley used the Pineapple Filling, page 147, but you can also try the Lemon Butter, page 131, or fill and frost with your favourite frosting.

6 egg whites
1 cup *(250 mL)* butter
2 cups *(500 mL)* sugar
1 tsp. *(5 mL)* vanilla
1½ tsp. *(7 mL)* almond flavouring
3 cups *(750 mL)* cake flour
3 tsp. *(15 mL)* baking powder
½ tsp. *(2 mL)* salt
1¼ cups *(310 mL)* milk

In a large bowl, with an electric mixer, beat the egg whites until stiff. Set aside.

Using the cake method, on page 10, in a separate large bowl, with an electric mixer, cream together the butter and sugar; add the flavourings. Sift the flour, baking powder and salt, and add alternately with the milk to the creamed mixture, beat until smooth.

Gently fold the egg whites into the cake batter. Pour into 2 or 3 greased round 9" (23 cm) cake pans.

Bake at 350°F (180°C) for 35 minutes. Test with a cake tester before removing from the oven. Cool.

Frost with Boiled Frosting on page 144.

Serves 8

Note: When my family was at home, I kept the layers in the freezer and used them one at a time for Baked Alaska.

A very simple ***Baked Alaska*** can be made by placing a frozen brick or mound of ice cream on the cake layer, making sure there is a border of cake around the ice cream. Refreeze on a baking sheet until just before serving. To serve, make meringue, pages 132 or 138, and spread a thick layer of meringue over the ice cream and the sides of the cake. Bake at 425°F (220°C) until the meringue is slightly browned, about 8 to 10 minutes. Watch carefully. Serve immediately.

Aunt Tilley *was my husband's aunt. She was jolly person who constantly struggled with her weight. She was such a good cook it was no wonder she had a weight problem. Her sense of humour and easygoing nature got her over the rough spots that are a part of every life. She was always so good to me, she became one of my favourite people.*

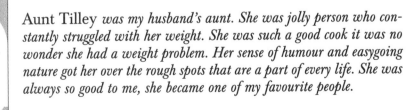

Pineapple Filling

2 tbsp. *(30 mL)* brown sugar
2 tbsp. *(30 mL)* flour
2, 14 oz. *(398 mL)* cans crushed
   pineapple
1 tbsp. *(15 mL)* butter

Combine the sugar and flour in a saucepan. Add the juice from the pineapple and bring to a boil. Simmer until thickened; add the pineapple and mix well. Remove from the heat. Add the butter and mix well. Allow to cool before filling the cake.

Yield : enough filling for a 3-layer 9" (23 cm) cake.

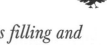

This filling and the Boiled Frosting, on page 144, made Aunt Tilley's white cake very special.

Seven-Minute Frosting

2 egg whites
1½ cups *(375 mL)* sugar
pinch of salt
¼ tsp. *(1 mL)* cream of tartar
⅓ cup *(75 mL)* water
2 tbsp. *(30 mL)* light corn syrup
1 tsp. *(5 mL)* vanilla

In the top of a double boiler, combine the egg whites, sugar, salt, cream of tartar, water and corn syrup. Beat with an electric hand mixer until thoroughly mixed. Place over boiling water in the bottom of the double boiler. Beat for 7 minutes, or until the frosting stands in stiff peaks. Beat in the vanilla.

Yield: sufficient for a 2-layer 9" (23 cm) cake

Fluffy, sweet and fat free, this classic frosting is often sprinkled with shredded sweetened coconut or chopped nuts after it has been spread over a cake.

Variations: For **Lemon Seven-Minute Frosting** substitute 3 tbsp. (45 mL) of fresh lemon juice for 3 tbsp. (45 mL) of the water. Add ¼ tsp. (1 mL) grated lemon rind.

For a **Brown Sugar (Penuche) Frosting**, substitute 1½ cups (375 mL) packed brown sugar for the white sugar and add ½ tsp. (2 mL) of maple flavouring with the vanilla.

Jiffy Devil's Food Cake

Dark, delicious and always moist.

1½ cups *(375 mL)* flour
1 cup *(250 mL)* sugar
3 tbsp. *(45 mL)* cocoa
½ tsp. *(2 mL)* salt
1 tsp. *(5 mL)* baking soda
1 tsp. *(5 mL)* vanilla
1 tsp. *(5 mL)* vinegar (scant)
½ cup *(125 mL)* vegetable oil
1 cup *(250 mL)* water

Put all of the dry ingredients into a mixing bowl. Make a little well in the centre and add the remaining ingredients. Beat well with an electric mixer.

Pour the batter into a 9 x 13" (23 x 33 cm) baking pan or 2, 9" (23 cm) layer cake pans. Bake at 350°F (180°C) for 30 minutes.

Frost with Chocolate Frosting, see below, or see the Baked Alaska note on page 146.

Serves 6 to 8, depending on whether or not my boys are around

HAZEL MCKEE *made this cake for my boys when they were little and, to this day, forty years later – they associate Hazel with chocolate cake. I could use the same recipe but, to them, Hazel's was far superior to mine.*

Chocolate Frosting

This icing is glossy, stays soft and doesn't run. Does it get any better than that?

6 oz. *(170 g)* unsweetened
   chocolate, melted
3 egg yolks
2¼ cups *(550 mL)* sugar
pinch of salt
¾ cup *(175 mL)* milk
2 tbsp. *(30 mL)* butter
2 tsp. *(10 mL)* vanilla

Melt the chocolate and set aside.

In a heavy saucepan, beat the egg yolks until thick, add sugar, salt, milk and butter. Cook over low heat, stirring constantly – do not let it stick!! Bring to a boil for 1 minute. Remove the frosting from the heat and stir in the chocolate and vanilla. Beat until it will spread nicely.

Yield: sufficient for a 9" (23 cm) layer cake.

Burnt Sugar Cake

Burnt Sugar:
1 cup *(250 mL)* white sugar
¾ cup (175 mL) boiling water

½ cup (125 mL) butter
¾ cup (175 mL) white sugar
2 eggs
¾ cup (175 mL) burnt sugar (see above)
1 tsp. *(5 mL)* vanilla
3 tsp. *(15 mL)* baking powder
pinch of salt
2 cups *(500 mL)* flour
¾ cup *(175 mL)* water

Burnt Sugar Frosting:
¼ cup *(60 mL)* burnt sugar
1 tbsp. *(15 mL)* soft butter
1½ cups *(375 mL)* icing (confectioners') sugar, more or less

Burnt Sugar: Put the white sugar in a heavy pan over medium heat. Stir it constantly. The sugar will clump as it browns, but eventually it will become a hot brown liquid with the scent of burnt sugar. You must work quickly and carefully, there is a very fine line between "not burnt enough" and "burnt too much".

Remove the pan from the heat and carefully pour in the boiling water. It will splatter, but keep stirring. Return the sugar to the heat and stir until all the lumps are gone. Do not over cook or you will have a hard glob of caramel. It should still be a liquid. Set aside to cool.

Cake: In a large bowl, with an electric mixer, cream together the butter, sugar and eggs until smooth.

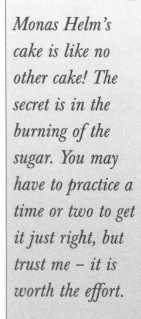

Monas Helm's cake is like no other cake! The secret is in the burning of the sugar. You may have to practice a time or two to get it just right, but trust me – it is worth the effort.

Add ¾ cup (174 mL) of the burnt sugar and the vanilla. Add the baking powder and salt to the flour. Add water and flour alternately to the creamed mixture, beating well after each addition, until all is mixed in. Pour into a 9 x 11" (23 x 33 cm) buttered cake pan and bake at 350°F (180°C) for 35 minutes. Cool and frost with burnt sugar frosting.

Frosting: Beat together the burnt sugar and butter. Gradually beat in the icing sugar until the consistency is suitable for spreading.

Serves 20

HAVE YOU *ever met someone and felt as though you have known them all your life? This is how people felt about Monas, she was like everybody's aunt. She took friendship very seriously. You never heard Monas say a bad word about anyone and she was generous to a fault.*

Lazy Daisy Oatmeal Cake

This cake by Kay Martin is moist and tasty. The mouthwatering aroma of the frosting under the broiler causes anticipation before realization.

1 cup *(250 mL)* oatmeal
1¼ cups *(310 mL)* boiling water

½ cup *(125 mL)* butter
1 cup *(250 mL)* white sugar
1 cup *(250 mL)* brown sugar
1 tsp. *(5 mL)* vanilla
2 eggs
1½ cups *(375 mL)* flour
pinch of salt
1 tsp. *(5 mL)* baking soda
1 tsp. *(5 mL)* cinnamon
½ tsp. *(2 mL)* nutmeg

Brown Sugar Coconut Frosting:
½ cup *(125 mL)* butter
1 cup *(250 mL)* brown sugar
3 tbsp. *(45 mL)* evaporated milk
½ cup *(125 mL)* chopped nuts
¾ cup *(175 mL)* sweetened
   shredded coconut

Soak the oats in boiling water for 20 minutes.

In a large bowl, with an electric mixer, cream together the butter, sugars, vanilla and eggs. Add the cooled oatmeal and mix thoroughly. Add the remaining ingredients and mix well. Pour the batter into a 9 x 13" (23 x 33 cm) pan and bake at 350°F (180°C) for 30 minutes.

Frosting: Gently bring the butter, sugar and milk to a boil. Simmer for 10 minutes – do not let it burn. Remove from the heat and stir in the nuts and coconut.

Remove the cake from the oven and pour the icing over evenly. Pop it back into the oven, under the broiler, for about 2 minutes. Watch carefully.

Serves 8

KAY, *my sister-in-law, was an excellent cook. She always searched out the best recipes. I don't know where she found time for research as she was the busiest person I ever knew. She had seven children, two large dogs (as in Great Danes) at least two cats, (every stray in the neighborhood found its way to Kay's doorstep,) and two turtles that grew so large they had to be given to the Aquarium. (Everybody else's 25-cent turtles died within days or weeks – Kay's thrived for years.) Working in the kitchen with Kay was always easy and fun. She made every move count, which is a gift.*

Taking a moment to reflect, I realize how blessed I was to have had such a delightful sister-in-law and good friend wrapped into one.

Carrot Cake

1 cup *(250 mL)* butter
1 cup *(250 mL)* brown sugar
1 cup *(250 mL)* white sugar
4 eggs
4 cups *(1 L)* grated carrots
2 tbsp. *(30 mL)* grated lemon rind
2 tbsp. *(30 mL)* grated orange rind
2 tbsp. *(30 mL)* lemon juice
2 tbsp. *(30 mL)* orange juice
2 oz. *(60 mL)* rum
3 cups *(750 mL)* flour
2 tsp. *(10 mL)* baking powder
1 tsp. *(5 mL) baking* soda
1 tsp. *(5 mL)* cinnamon
½ tsp. *(2 mL)* salt
1 cup *(250 mL)* chopped raisins
1 cup *(250 mL)* chopped pecans

Cream Cheese Frosting:
8 oz. *(250 g)* cream cheese, room
    temperature
1 tbsp. *(15 mL)* lemon juice
1 tsp. *(5 mL)* grated lemon rind
1½ cups *(375 mL)* icing
    (confectioners') sugar, more or
    less

In a large bowl, with an electric mixer, cream together the butter, sugars, eggs, carrots, rind, juices and rum.

Combine the dry ingredients and beat into the creamed mixture. Stir in the raisins and pecans.

Pour the batter into a greased, parchment-paper-lined 11 x 15 x 3" (28 x 38 x 8 cm). The round 12 x 4" (30 x 10 cm) or 14 x 4" (35 x 10 cm) wedding cake pans also work well.

Bake at 350°F (180°C) for 1 hour. Check with a cake tester before removing the cake from the oven. Cool before frosting.

Frosting: With an electric mixer, beat the cream cheese until fluffy. Beat in the lemon juice and rind. Gradually beat in the icing sugar until the consistency is suitable for spreading.

Serves 30

This is the recipe we used for Dad's ninetieth birthday. I was probably a little generous with the rum – it was more like 2 good "gluggs" then 2 oz.! This cake is moist and full of flavour from the orange and lemon juices and zest – a real family standby.

Note: This cake freezes very well. You may make it ahead and freeze it. Frost it the day you serve it.

Variations: If you like a **Spicy Carrot Cake**, add ½ tsp. (2 mL) EACH of ground nutmeg, allspice and cloves WITH the cinnamon.

Gingerbread

Remember this treat? This recipe is my Granny Olsen's, but gingerbread has been a long-time favourite – since the middle ages according to one source, for thousands of years according to others. Gingerbread is very versatile, you can add grated lemon or orange rind, a spoonful of brandy, chopped nuts and additional minced candied ginger or grated fresh ginger.

½ cup *(125 mL)* butter
½ cup *(125 mL)* sugar
1 egg
½ cup *(125 mL)* light molasses
1½ cups *(375 mL)* flour
½ tsp. *(2 mL)* salt
¾ tsp. *(3 mL)* baking soda
½ tsp. *(2 mL)* ground ginger
½ tsp. *(2 mL)* cinnamon
½ cup *(125 mL)* boiling water

In a large bowl, with an electric mixer, cream together the butter and sugar. Stir in the egg and molasses, then the wet and dry ingredients alternately. Do not over mix.

Pour the batter into a buttered 8" (20 cm) square baking pan. Bake at 350°F (180°C) for 40 minutes.

You can top gingerbread with a variety of sauces, anything from whipped cream to applesauce, a custard sauce, lemon sauce, Rum Sauce, page 127, or Brown Sugar Sauce, page 127.

Serves 6

GRANNY *brought many strange ideas with her from Denmark. Today we might call them superstitions – but you didn't dare use that word in front of her. To Granny it was basic knowledge; superstition had no place in it! I can't remember most of them, but one is etched forever in my mind. A bird pecking at your window was a sure sign that some-one in the family was going to die. Well, one day a little sparrow landed on the sill and pecked vigorously on the glass before he could be banished. Granny was beside herself for the rest of the day – not quite in tears, but almost – sure that the next time to town there would be bad news from Denmark. The next morning, via "party line" tele-phone, we received the message that my uncle's wife had died suddenly the night before, of a ruptured appendix? True Story! I didn't actually become a believer at that point, but please don't laugh at me if you see me pound on the window, chasing away a bird.*

Crumb Cake

1 cup *(250 mL)* white sugar
2 cups *(500 mL)* flour
¾ cup *(175 mL)* butter

1 cup *(250 mL)* sour milk OR
   buttermilk
1 egg
1 tsp. *(5 mL)* baking soda
1 tsp. *(5 mL)* cloves
1 tsp. *(5 mL)* cinnamon
1 cup *(250 mL)* chopped yellow
   raisins (optional)

In a large bowl, make crumbs by combining the sugar and flour, then cut in the butter until the mixture resembles coarse crumbs.

Reserve 1 cup (250 mL) of crumbs for the topping. To the remaining crumbs, with an electric mixer, beat in the rest of the ingredients in the order given, except the raisins. Stir in the raisins.

Pour the batter into a buttered 9 x 13" (23 x 33 cm) cake pan. Spread the reserved cup of crumbs evenly over the surface. Bake at 325°F (160℃) for 25 minutes.

Serves 8

Aunt Edith's Crumb Cake was the "quick cake" of the day – like a cake mix today.

Rhubarb Coffee Cake

½ cup *(125 mL)* butter
1½ cups *(375 mL)* brown sugar
1 egg
1 tsp. *(5 mL)* vanilla
pinch of salt
1 tsp. *(5 mL)* baking soda
2 cups *(500 mL)* flour
1 cup *(250 mL)* buttermilk
2 cups *(500 mL)* coarsely chopped
   red rhubarb

2 tbsp. *(30 mL)* sugar
½ tsp. *(2 mL)* cinnamon

In a large bowl, with an electric mixer, cream together the butter, sugar, egg and vanilla.

In a separate bowl, combine the salt, soda and flour. Stir the dry ingredients and the buttermilk alternately into the creamed mixture, about half of each at a time. Stir in the rhubarb last.

Pour into a buttered 9 x 13" (23 x 33 cm) cake pan. Combine sugar and cinnamon and sprinkle over the batter. Bake at 325°F (160℃) for 50 minutes.

Serves 8

Aunt Hazel used to drive us wild with the heavenly smell of Rhubarb Coffee Cake in the middle of the afternoon. Suppertime seemed an eternity away.

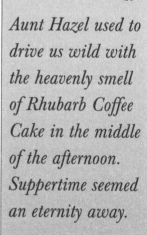

Note: This cake is best fresh because the rhubarb can change colour when frozen, from a pretty pink to a tasteless grey. If you use any other fruit, e.g., apples – it is freezeable.

153

Banana Loaf

At our house, Banana Loaf is considered comfort food. I always have Banana Loaf in the deep freeze. I use up any ripe bananas to make the cake and pop it into the freezer. There always seem to be bananas to use up. This recipe can also be used for muffins.

½ cup *(125 mL)* butter
1 cup *(250 mL)* sugar
1 egg
1½ very ripe medium bananas
1 tsp. *(5 mL)* almond flavouring
2 cups *(500 mL)* flour
2 tsp. *(10 mL)* baking powder
½ tsp. *(2 mL)* baking soda
pinch of salt
¾ cup *(175 mL)* sour milk

In a large bowl, with an electric mixer, cream together the butter, sugar, egg, banana and almond flavouring.

In a separate bowl, combine the flour, baking powder, baking soda and the salt. Beat the dry and wet ingredients, alternately, into the banana mixture.

Pour the batter into a well-buttered 5 x 9 x 3" (13 x 23 x 8 cm) loaf pan.

Bake at 350°F (160°C) for 50 to 60 minutes, or until done. Test with a cake tester before removing from the oven. Tester should come out dry.

Serves 10

Variations: For **Banana Pecan Loaf**, stir in ½ cup (125 mL) chopped pecans just before pouring the batter into the loaf pan. Vanilla may be substituted for the almond flavouring. 1 cup (250 mL) of packed brown sugar may be substituted for the white sugar and, if you are feeling really daring, add a dash of ground nutmeg.

Note: Rich in potassium and Vitamin C, bananas are also low in fat.

Remember that you must not vigorously beat the batter of cakes, muffins or cookies after you have added the flour. Beat it just enough to mix all the ingredients thoroughly, that is all. If you over beat the batter – you toughen it.

Chocolate Banana Loaf

¾ cup *(175 mL)* butter
1⅔ cups *(400 mL)* sugar
2 eggs
1¼ cups *(310 mL)* mashed banana
1 tsp. *(5 mL)* vanilla
2 cups *(500 mL)* flour
¾ cup *(175 mL)* cocoa
1½ tsp. *(7 mL)* baking soda
pinch of salt
⅔ cup *(150 mL)* milk
1 tsp. *(5 mL)* vinegar

Chocolate Banana Frosting:
¼ cup *(60 mL)* butter
½ cup *(125 mL)* mashed banana
2 tbsp. *(30 mL)* milk
1 tsp. *(5 mL)* vanilla
½ cup *(125 mL)* cocoa
3 cups *(750 mL)* icing
   (confectioners') sugar

In a large bowl, with an electric mixer, cream together the butter, sugar, eggs, banana and vanilla.

In a separate bowl, combine the flour, cocoa, soda and salt. Beat the wet and dry ingredients, alternately, into the banana mixture.

This is large enough for 2, 5 x 9 x 3" (13 x 23 x 8 cm) loaf pans or a 9 x 13" (23 x 33 cm) cake pan. Pour the batter into the buttered pan(s).

Bake at 350°F (180°C) for 50 to 60 minutes, or until the top springs back. Test with a cake tester before removing from oven. Cake tester should come out dry. Cool the cake before frosting it.

Frosting: Beat together the butter, banana, milk and vanilla, then add the cocoa. Add the icing sugar gradually, beating until the desired consistency is reached.

This loaf freezes well. Freeze unfrosted and frost before serving.

Serves 10

Banana Loaf is comfort food – this may be gilding the lily, but a little added comfort is always appreciated. Judy, Tracey's mom, introduced this loaf to us as the perfect way to eat bananas.

Don't open the oven door on cakes, soufflés, puff pastry, cream puffs, bread, anything that is rising. Keep the oven door closed until it is almost time to remove them from the oven.

Light Fruitcake

In my opinion, Kim Quan's light fruitcake is the very best light fruitcake recipe. However, every person I meet thinks theirs is the best! Almond Paste and Royal Icing may be used to decorate this cake. They also seal in moisture and flavour, so ice the cakes before storing them.

2 lbs. *(1 kg)* light raisins
3 lbs. *(1.5 kg)* red glacé cherries
3 lbs. *(1.5 kg)* glacé deluxe mixed fruit*
1 lb. *(500 g)* glacé pineapple
2 lbs. *(1 kg)* pecans
2 lbs. *(1 kg)* almonds
2 tbsp. *(30 mL)* candied ginger
2 cups *(500 mL)* pear brandy**
1 cup *(250 mL)* corn syrup

8 cups *(2 L)* flour
2 lbs. *(1 kg)* butter
5 cups *(1.25 L)* brown sugar
1 tbsp. *(15 mL)* salt
16 eggs, separated
4 tbsp. *(60 mL)* vanilla

* Buy good-quality fruit in larger pieces for the best flavour.

** It must be Pear, do not substitute.

This is a large recipe and it requires 3, 9 x 9 x 4" (23 x 23 x 10 cm) pans. Fruitcake pans or wedding cake pans or large roasting pans will all work. Shiny metal pans are best – to help prevent over browning. Line pans with parchment paper, greasing the pans is not necessary if parchment paper is used.

Chop all the fruit very finely. (Do not use a food processor.) Soak the fruit overnight in the pear brandy and syrup. In the morning, dredge flour into the fruit mixture.

With an electric mixer, cream the butter, sugar, salt, egg yolks and vanilla, and stir into the fruit. Wash the beaters very well and, in a separate bowl, beat egg whites until very stiff. Fold carefully (not using a heavy hand) into the fruit and batter mixture.

Pour the batter into prepared fruitcake pans and bake at 275°F (140°C) for 3 hours. Test with a cake tester before removing the cakes from the oven. Cool 30 to 60 minutes before removing from the pans.

To store the completely cooled cakes, ice them with Almond Paste, page 157, and Royal Icing, page 168. Wrap them in clean brandy-soaked cloths and then in plastic wrap or heavy resealable plastic bags. Do Not use aluminum foil directly on the cake as the brandy/fruit combination can dissolve the foil!

Yield: about 15 to 18 lbs. (7 to 8 kg) of fruitcake

OUR FRIEND *Dick Quan went back to Hong Kong for six months and returned with a beautiful, sparkly-eyed wife, Kim. The only word she knew in English was "Hi". That was enough, we became lifelong friends. Kim had impeccable taste in all things, not the least, food. She had a passion for this fruitcake and every year we made a three-day project – one day for chopping, one for baking, one for icing and putting away. Good times!*

Dark Fruitcake

7 lbs. *(3 kg)* mixed glacéed and dried fruit: dates, prunes, raisins, apricots and currants
2 lbs. *(1 kg)* mincemeat (4 cups)
2 lbs. *(1 kg)* nuts: pecans, almonds, cashews, walnuts
1 cup *(250 mL)* dark rum
1 cup *(250 mL)* cognac

8 cups *(2 L)* flour
1 tsp. *(5 mL)* salt
1 lb. *(500 g)* butter
2 cups *(500 mL)* white sugar
3 cups *(750 mL)* brown sugar
12 eggs
3 tbsp. *(45 mL)* vanilla
1½ tbsp. *(30 mL)* instant coffee granules
½ cup *(125 mL)* light molasses
1 tsp. *(5 mL)* EACH allspice, cloves, nutmeg, cinnamon
2 tbsp. *(30 mL)* baking powder

Choose cake pans and line them with parchment paper. Use 3, 9 x 9 x 4" (23 x 23 x 10 cm) fruitcake pans or wedding cake pans. Large shallow roasting pans are an alternative, as are a combination of smaller ones. Baking time will vary for smaller pans.

Chop the fruit and nuts fairly finely (not in a food processor). Soak the fruit overnight in the liquor. The next day, dredge the flour and salt into the fruit.

With an electric mixer, cream the salt, butter, sugars, eggs, vanilla, coffee, molasses, spices and baking powder. Stir into the fruit and flour mixture.

Pour the batter into the prepared pans. Bake at 275°F (140°C) for 3 hours. Test with a cake tester before removing from the oven.

Yield: about 15 to 18 lbs. (7 to 8 kg) of fruitcake

There are three different types of people: those that like dark fruitcake, those that like light fruitcake, and those that don't like any fruitcake. If you are a dark fruitcake person, this is the recipe for you.

Note: See the cooling and storage information on page 156. We prefer this cake without icing.

Almond Paste

3 x 7½ oz. *(245 g)* pkgs. almond paste
3 tbsp. *(45 mL)* corn syrup or honey

Knead the almond paste until it is soft enough to roll. Roll it out to the desired size. Spread 1 tbsp. (15 mL) of syrup on the top surface of each fruitcake. Place one-third of the almond paste (1 pkg.) on the top of each cake. Pat down. Ice the top and sides with Royal Icing, page 168.

Yield: will ice 3, 9 x 9 x 4" (23 x 23 x 10 cm) cakes

Lemon Bars

A refreshing delight for those of us who love lemon! The buttery shortbread base is a perfect foil for the tangy lemon topping.

Shortbread Base:
2½ cups *(625 mL)* flour
1¼ cups *(310 mL)* butter
¾ cup *(175 mL)* icing
(confectioners') sugar

Lemon Topping:
5 eggs
2½ cups *(625 mL)* sugar
½ cup *(125 mL)* lemon juice
1 tsp. *(5 mL)* grated lemon rind
⅓ cup *(75 mL)* flour
¼ tsp. *(1 mL)* baking powder
pinch of salt

icing (confectioners') sugar for
dusting

Combine the flour and sugar and cut in the butter until the mixture resembles coarse crumbs. Press into a 11 x 17" (28 x 43 cm) cookie/jelly roll pan.

Bake at 350°F (180°C) for 15 to 20 minutes. Let cool.

With an electric mixer, beat the eggs, sugar, lemon juice and rind, flour, baking powder and salt. Pour over the crumb crust.

Bake at 350°F (180°C) for 25 minutes. Dust with icing sugar while still hot. Cut into fingers instead of squares.

Yield: 48 pieces

WHEN *my granddaughter Amanda was little she liked to make Lemon Bars. I don't think it was so much the flavour as the colour. Yellow was her favourite. One spring day Amanda and I went to the greenhouse and chose the flowers for the patio pots. She chose her own flower. It was no surprise that it was bright yellow. We hurried home and planted them before they could wilt. The planting completed – we went into the kitchen to make the Lemon Bars (her suggestion). Together, we finally put the pan into the oven.*

While I was cleaning up, Amanda wandered out onto the patio, and came back in tears, screaming "MY YELLOW FLOWER FELL OVER!" I replied, "Your yellow flower couldn't fall over, Amanda." "Yes! Yes, my yellow flower FELL OVER." Tears ran like rivers down her little cheeks. I dried my hands and went to see what had happened, expecting to see a thirsty, wilted, yellow flower. However, the yellow flower was on the ground, along with every other flower we had planted that morning. My dear old dog Jake had systematically gone from pot to pot – pulled out each and every flower and dropped them, unharmed, onto the patio. We dried the tears and busied ourselves putting our flowers back where they belonged. In so doing we almost forgot the Lemon Bars in the oven. It was one of those days . . . !

Gooey Caramel Bars

Chocolate Base:
1 cup *(250 mL)* butter
1 cup *(250 mL)* white sugar
2 eggs
1½ cups *(375 mL)* flour
1 tbsp. *(15 mL)* cocoa

Caramel Filling:
¾ cup *(175 mL)* butter
1½ cups *(375 mL)* brown sugar
10 oz. *(300 mL)* can sweetened
    condensed milk
4 tbsp. *(60 mL)* flour

Butter Frosting:
6 tbsp. *(90 mL)* butter
7 tbsp. *(105 mL)* icing
    (confectioners') sugar
2 tbsp. *(30 mL)* milk
2 tbsp. *(30 mL)* boiling water
1 tsp. *(5 mL)* vanilla

Base: Cream the butter, sugar and eggs, then beat in the flour and cocoa. Spread into a 11 x 17" (28 x 43 cm) cookie pan. Bake at 350°F (180°C) for 12 minutes.

Filling: Put the butter, sugar, condensed milk and flour into the top of a double boiler and heat to a slow bubble. Pour the filling over the hot base and pop it back into the oven until it just barely bubbles, about 2 to 3 minutes. (If you bake it too much it gets very hard — so be careful.) Cool.

Frosting: Put all of the ingredients in a mixing bowl and beat very well with an electric mixer. Do not under beat. When the frosting is very smooth, pour it evenly over the filling.

These bars freeze well.

Yield: 40 pieces

Note: This frosting may seem to curdle or separate, but the beating smooths it out and makes it manageable.

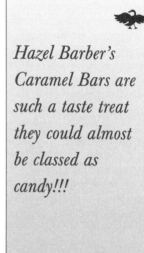

Hazel Barber's Caramel Bars are such a taste treat they could almost be classed as candy!!!

HAZEL *is a friend from Medicine Hat. I call her often and when I say, "How are you today, Hazel?" Her quick reply is, "Perfect!" I can't help but laugh. It always pleases me to know that I have at least one friend in this crazy world who is "perfect".*

Pecan Squares

This square is rich and should have a warning label attached – "Incredibly delicious – eat at your own risk – could be addictive!"

Shortbread Base:
2 cups *(500 mL)* flour
½ cup *(125 mL)* icing
    (confectioners') sugar
1 cup *(250 mL)* butter

Pecan Topping:
¾ cup *(175 mL)* brown sugar
¾ cup *(175 mL)* honey
6 tbsp. *(90 mL)* whipping cream
2 cups *(500 mL)* chopped pecans
1 tsp. *(5 mL)* vanilla

Pictured on page 175.

Base: Combine the flour and sugar. With an electric mixer, mix in the butter until the mixture resembles coarse crumbs.

Press into a buttered 9 x 13" (23 x 33 cm) pan. Bake at 350°F (180°C) for 20 minutes.

Topping: In a heavy saucepan, combine the brown sugar, honey and cream. Bring to a boil and simmer for 2 minutes. Add the chopped nuts and bring to a boil again for 1 minute. Remove from the heat and stir in the vanilla.

Pour the topping over the base and spread evenly. Bake for 20 minutes. Cool. Cut into squares while still a little warm.

These squares freeze well.

Yield: 24 pieces

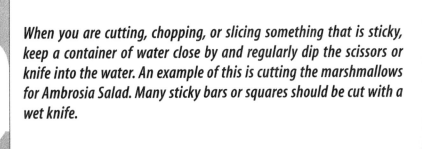

When you are cutting, chopping, or slicing something that is sticky, keep a container of water close by and regularly dip the scissors or knife into the water. An example of this is cutting the marshmallows for Ambrosia Salad. Many sticky bars or squares should be cut with a wet knife.

Chocolate Mint Bars

Chocolate Base:
Jiffy Devil's Food Cake, see page 148

Mint Filling:
1 tbsp. *(15 mL)* gelatin (1 env.)
¼ cup *(60 mL)* boiling water
1 cup *(250 mL)* butter
4 cups *(1 L)* icing (confectioners')
    sugar
few drops mint liqueur (green)

Chocolate Frosting:
8 oz. *(250 g)* semisweet chocolate
3 tbsp. *(45 mL)* butter

Base: Prepare the Devil's Food Cake batter and pour into a 10 x 15" (25 x 38 cm) jelly roll/cookie pan.

Bake at 350°F (180°C) for 10 minutes. Let cool.

Filling: Soften the gelatin in the boiling water. Cream the butter and icing sugar with an electric mixer. Add the gelatin and mix well. Drizzle in a few drops of green mint liqueur – just enough to make it a pale green colour. Spread the filling evenly over the cooled cake.

Frosting: Melt the chocolate and butter in the top of a double boiler. Pour evenly over the filling.

These bars freeze well.

Yield: 35 pieces

My granddaughter Tracey and I created this recipe many years ago. It is a family favourite.

WHEN *my granddaughter Tracey was about eleven, she caught the measles. She was not ill, but had enough spots to keep her home from school Happily she was to spend the week with me. What a break for me!*

Tracey was not one to sit around and do nothing. She got the notion that she wanted to learn how to knit. Good plan. We dug out some wool and started knitting a vest for her. One day, to take a little break from the knitting, we started flipping through magazines and came up with this recipe. Together we whipped it up. To our delight, the cake was a winner, and the vest, when finished, not only fit, but looked very chic. All in all – the week was one for a grandma to keep in her heart forever!!

Peanut Butter Bars

My daughter-in-law Ellen can always be counted on to find scrumptious recipes. This is one. These are truly deluxe Rice Krispie cakes – a whole new dimension.

Crunchy Peanut Butter Base:
1 cup *(250 mL)* brown sugar
1 cup *(250 mL)* corn syrup
2 cups *(500 mL)* smooth or chunky peanut butter
1 tsp. *(5 mL)* vanilla
2 cups *(500 mL)* Rice Krispies
4 cups *(1 L)* Corn Flakes
½ cup *(125 mL)* chopped unsalted peanuts

Brown Sugar Frosting:
¾ cup *(175 mL)* brown sugar
2 tbsp. *(30 mL)* butter
3 tbsp. *(45 mL)* whipping cream
icing (confectioners') sugar to thicken

Base: In a heavy saucepan, combine the sugar, syrup, peanut butter and vanilla. Melt over low heat. Bring to a boil and cook until the sugar is dissolved.

Remove from the heat and stir in the Rice Krispies, Corn Flakes and chopped peanuts. Mix well and press into a 9 x 13" (23 x 33 cm) pan.

Frosting: With an electric mixer, cream the sugar and butter. Add the cream and beat until smooth. Gradually beat in the icing sugar until it is a good spreading consistency. Spread over the base and cut into bars or squares.

These freeze very well.

Yield: 30 pieces

Variation: If you love chocolate with peanut butter, omit the Brown Sugar Frosting and melt 3 to 4 squares (85 to 115 g) of semisweet chocolate and spread the melted chocolate over the peanut butter base.

ELLEN IS MORE *like a daughter – we think alike and work well together. We have had many experiences together that we can look back on and laugh. One that comes to mind is a trip to Chicago. We were lucky enough to be in a hotel just a few blocks from the Water Tower (a wonderful place to shop). By 11 a.m. Ellen had blisters on her feet from her beautiful but impractical shoes. Did that deter her? No way. We simply bought her a pair of running shoes, along with ointment, gauze and tape. We rushed back to the hotel and I bandaged up her sore feet. She put on the running shoes and we rushed back to cover the unseen, unshopped portion of the Water Tower. We had a great day. (You realize, of course, that we do not get to Chicago often.)*

Matrimonial Cake

Date Filling:
2 cups *(500 mL)* dried, pitted, chopped dates
1 cup *(250 mL)* boiling water
2 tbsp. *(30 mL)* brown sugar
½ lemon, juice and grated rind of

Rolled Oat Layer:
1 cup *(250 mL)* butter
1 cup *(250 mL)* brown sugar
1 tsp. *(5 mL)* vanilla
1½ cups *(375 mL)* rolled oats
1½ cups *(375 mL)* flour
1 tsp. *(5 mL)* baking soda

Filling: In a heavy saucepan, cook the dates and water slowly, until smooth. Stir in the brown sugar, lemon juice and rind. (You may have to add a little more water to get a smooth texture.) Set aside to cool

Cream the butter, sugar and vanilla. Stir in the oats, flour and baking soda.

Press ⅔ of the oat mixture into a well-buttered 9 x 13" (23 x 33 cm) pan. Spread the dates evenly over the base. Sprinkle the rest of the oat mixture over the dates and press down ever so gently.

Bake at 350°F (180°C) until light brown, about 30 minutes.

This freezes very well.

Yield: 36 squares

Variations: The date filling may also be used as a filling for oatmeal cookies.

Chopped dried figs, prunes or apricots may be substituted for the dates. Add ½ cup (125 mL) of brown sugar if using fruits other than dates. Add ½ cup (125 mL) chopped pecans or walnuts, if you want a nutty flavour.

Half dates and half raisins, cooked together, make a delicious filling.

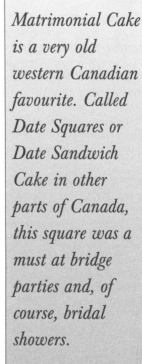

Matrimonial Cake is a very old western Canadian favourite. Called Date Squares or Date Sandwich Cake in other parts of Canada, this square was a must at bridge parties and, of course, bridal showers.

Date & Nut Bar

Healthy, but sinfully good, what more do you want!

1 cup *(250 mL)* coarsely chopped nuts: pecans, walnuts, hazelnuts, etc.
1 cup *(250 mL)* dried, pitted, chopped dates
2 eggs
1 cup *(250 mL)* brown sugar
1 tsp. *(5 mL)* vanilla
5 tbsp. *(75 mL)* flour
½ tsp. *(2 mL)* baking powder
pinch of salt

1 tbsp. *(15 mL)* icing (confectioners') sugar

Coarsely chop the nuts and dates and set aside.

In a large bowl, with an electric mixer, beat the eggs until thick. Add the brown sugar and vanilla. Beat in the flour and baking powder. Mix well. Stir in the dates and nuts.

Pour into a buttered 9 x 13" (23 x 33 cm) pan. Bake at 325°F (160°C) for 30 minutes.

Sprinkle icing sugar, through a sieve, over the cake while it is hot.

This freezes well.

Yield: 24 pieces

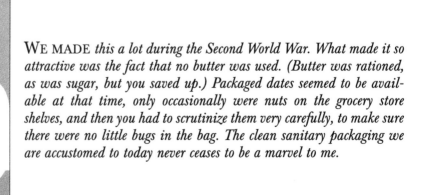

WE MADE *this a lot during the Second World War. What made it so attractive was the fact that no butter was used. (Butter was rationed, as was sugar, but you saved up.) Packaged dates seemed to be available at that time, only occasionally were nuts on the grocery store shelves, and then you had to scrutinize them very carefully, to make sure there were no little bugs in the bag. The clean sanitary packaging we are accustomed to today never ceases to be a marvel to me.*

Cookies
&
Candies

Rosettes

A rosette iron is a must for these delicate Scandinavian pastries. The iron is comprised of a long metal rod with a heatproof handle and several options for the rosettes, e.g., stars, flowers, hearts, etc. Vi Lust's recipe is easy to follow and makes lovely rosettes.

1 cup *(250 mL)* flour
½ cup *(125 mL)* evaporated milk
½ cup *(125 mL)* water
1½ tsp. *(7 mL)* sugar
pinch of salt
2 eggs
1 tsp. *(5 mL)* vegetable oil
2 tsp. *(10 mL)* lemon juice

fat or oil for deep-frying

1 cup *(250 mL)* sugar OR cinnamon
    sugar

Put the rosette iron in the fat as it is heating.

The simplest way to make the Rosette batter is to put all of the ingredients, except the oil for deep-frying and the last amount of sugar, into a blender or food processor. Mix thoroughly, until very smooth. It should be a runny batter – very much like crêpe batter.

The biggest secret in frying rosettes is that the iron must be hot, so that the batter will stick to the iron.

To start – pat the hot iron on a paper towel to remove excess oil. Submerge the iron into the batter, halfway to the top of the rosette. (If you plunged it in all the way – you would never get the rosette off.) So, half submerge the iron into the batter – then submerge it into the hot fat.

When the rosette is crisp and lightly browned, remove it from the hot fat – with very little pressure it will pop off onto a paper towel.

Sprinkle immediately with cinnamon sugar.

Go on to the next one. It gets easier as you get more experience.

These freeze well.

Yield: 3 dozen

Pictured on page 175

Shortbread

2 cups/1 lb. *(500 mL)* butter
1 cup *(250 mL)* icing (confectioners')
   sugar
½ cup *(125 mL)* cornstarch
pinch of salt
1 tsp. *(5 mL)* vanilla
3 cups *(750 mL)* flour

In a mixing bowl, with an electric mixer, cream the butter and sugar together until the colour is a pale yellow. Beat in the cornstarch, salt and vanilla. Beat in the flour 1 cup (250 mL) at a time. Do not over beat once you have added the flour as it toughens the shortbread.

A cookie press works well for shortbread, however, rolling out the chilled dough and using your favourite cookie cutters is an easy alternative.

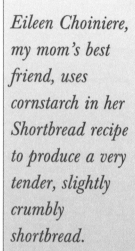

Eileen Choiniere, my mom's best friend, uses cornstarch in her Shortbread recipe to produce a very tender, slightly crumbly shortbread.

Bake at 350°F (180°C) for 10 to 12 minutes. You want hardly a hint of brown on the edges, if any. Watch carefully.

Yield: 7 dozen cookies

Pictured on page 175.

Variations:

For **Lemon Shortbread**, omit the vanilla and add 2 tsp. (10 mL) lemon juice and 2 tsp. (10 mL) grated lemon peel.

For **Ginger Shortbread**, stir in ¾ cup (175 mL) minced candied or crystallized ginger.

For **Chocolate Shortbread**, melt 3 oz. (85 g) semisweet chocolate and cool slightly. Stir into the batter and bake as above.

For **Brown Sugar Shortbread**, substitute brown sugar for the icing (confectioners') sugar.

Sugar Cookies

This was the only cookie I was aware of until I was about seven. Sometimes Granny Olsen would put some jam in between some of these cookies, but that made them soft. I liked them crisp. This basic recipe is ideal for making shaped, decorated Christmas, Valentine, Halloween, etc., cookies. Decorate with Cookie Paint or Royal Icing.

2 cups/1 lb. *(500 g)* butter
1½ cups *(375 mL)* sugar
2 eggs
2 tsp. *(10 mL)* vanilla
2 tsp. *(10 mL)* baking soda
2 tsp. *(10 mL)* cream of tartar
pinch of salt
5 cups *(1.25 L)* flour

In a large bowl, with an electric mixer, cream butter and sugar. Add eggs and vanilla. Work in baking soda, cream of tartar, salt and flour. Refrigerate dough for 1 hour.

Roll out the dough to ¼" (1 cm) thick and cut with 2" (5 cm) or 3" (8 cm) cookie cutters. Bake at 325°F (160°C) for 10 to12 minutes, until the edges are just barely brown. Watch carefully.

Yield: 6 dozen cookies

Variation: Sprinkle cinnamon sugar on the cookies just before baking.

For **Cookie Paint**, combine 2 cups (500 mL) of icing sugar with 2 tbsp. (30 mL) water, or more for desired consistency. To make several colours, divide the icing sugar mixture into small bowls, add colour. Cover with plastic wrap to keep it moist. Add a bit of water if the paint dries out.

Royal Icing

3 egg whites
½ tsp. *(2 mL)* cream of tartar
1 tsp. *(5 mL)* vanilla
1 tbsp. *(15 mL)* lemon juice
2 tbsp. *(30 mL)* glycerin
1 lb. *(500 g)* icing (confectioners')
   sugar (4-5 cups *[1-1.25 L]*)

With an electric mixer, beat the egg whites and cream of tartar until frothy. Add vanilla, lemon juice, glycerin and icing sugar. Beat until peaks form. If it is too thin add icing sugar; if it is too thick add a few drops of water. Work quickly and keep the bowl covered with a damp cloth to prevent crusting.

For fruitcakes, ice top and sides with Royal Icing. For cookies, use a metal spatula for spreading and a small pastry tip for decorating.

Yield: about 3 cups (750 mL) of icing

Granny had a large crockery churn in the pantry that she kept filled with these Sugar Cookies. She was always prepared for visitors. Looking back – I wonder if visitors happened by more than a half dozen times a year, but Granny was always ready!! Grandpa and I were always happy about the never-ending cookie supply.

Ginger Stacks

½ cup *(125 mL)* butter
⅔ cup *(150 mL)* brown sugar
½ cup *(125 mL)* molasses
1 egg
1 tbsp. *(15 mL)* vinegar
2 tsp. *(10 mL)* vanilla
3 cups *(750 mL)* flour
¾ tsp. *(3 mL)* ground ginger
¾ tsp. *(3 mL)* baking soda
¾ tsp. *(3 mL)* cinnamon
pinch of salt
½ tsp. *(2 mL)* cloves
¼ tsp. *(1 mL)* cardamom

Ginger Filling:

2½ cups *(625 mL)* icing
   (confectioners') sugar
3 tbsp. *(45 mL)* finely chopped
   crystallized ginger
4 tbsp. *(60 mL)* ginger marmalade
4 tbsp. *(60 mL)* butter
4 tbsp. *(60 mL)* Grand Marnier OR
   orange juice

In a large bowl, with an electric mixer, cream the butter and sugar together. Beat in the molasses, egg, vinegar and vanilla; mix well. Beat in the dry ingredients. Chill the dough overnight or for 3 to 4 hours.

Roll out the dough thinly and cut with a cookie cutter. Place on greased cookie sheets and bake at 325°F (160°C) for 10 to 12 minutes. Cool.

Filling: Put all of the ingredients into a large bowl. With an electric mixer, beat until smooth. Spread the filling on half of the cookies. Press the remaining cookies on top.

These cookies freeze well.

Yield: 3 dozen stacked

Pictured on page 175.

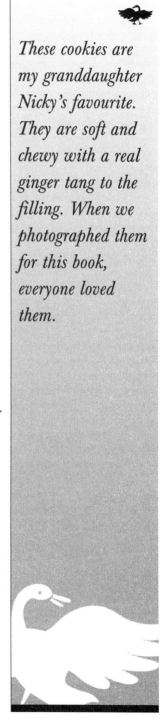

These cookies are my granddaughter Nicky's favourite. They are soft and chewy with a real ginger tang to the filling. When we photographed them for this book, everyone loved them.

A FEW *days after the purchase of my new car (which had a sun roof as well as many buttons), my granddaughters Nicole and Amanda joined me one afternoon for lunch, followed by shopping. When we got back to the car it was unbearably hot, so Nicole opened the sun roof, turned on the air conditioning as well, and the CD player. We headed for home singing the Unicorn song with the Irish Rovers. Life was good. I stopped for gas, and decided on a car wash. You're right. We forgot about the sun roof, until a blast of ice-cold water poured over Nikki and me. As we desperately tried to find the right button to shut the roof, screaming at the top of our lungs, Amanda screamed, "The Soap is coming! The Soap is coming! It's BLUE – It's BLUE!! We barely got the sunroof shut before the blue soap got us. It's not an experience I would repeat, however, we spent the rest of the day, and many hours since, laughing at our foolishness. Now, when the girls get in the car, they ask right away, "Are we going to the car wash?"*

Date-Filled Oatmeal Wafers

These soft, chewy wafers are my husband Doug's favourite cookie. For that reason, I always keep some of them hidden in the deep freeze for a "time of need". A "time of need" is when the garage needs to be cleaned, the leaves need to be raked, or the snow needs to be shovelled!

Date Filling:

26 oz. *(750 g)* pkg., pitted, chopped
   dates
boiling water to just cover dates
1 tbsp. *(15 mL)* sugar
1 tbsp. *(15 mL)* lemon juice

Oatmeal Wafers:

2 cups/1 lb. *(500 mL)* butter
2 cups *(500 mL)* brown sugar
3 cups *(750 mL)* rolled oats
4 cups *(1 L)* flour
2 tsp. *(10 mL)* baking soda
½ tsp. *(2 mL)* salt

Filling: This comes first. In a small heavy saucepan, combine the dates and water – make sure there is enough water – but don't drown the dates. Heat slowly, stirring often. When soft, add the sugar and lemon juice. Remove from the heat and set aside.

Wafers: In a large bowl, with an electric mixer, cream together the butter and sugar. Stir in the dry ingredients. You may have to add a few drops of water to the dough to make it the right consistency to roll.

Roll out the dough thinly and cut with a 2½" (6 cm) or 3" (8 cm) cookie cutter.

Place the cookies on greased cookie sheets and bake at 350°F (180°C) for 10 to 12 minutes, until just a little brown around the edges. Do not over bake.

When the cookies are cooled, spread the date mixture on 1 cookie and cover with another. Pinch them together. Repeat until all the cookies are filled. If you have more date filling than cookies – use the balance on graham wafers.

These cookies freeze very well.

Yield: 6 dozen filled cookies

Pictured on page 175.

Amandines

½ cup *(125 mL)* butter
½ cup *(125 mL)* finely chopped or
   ground toasted almonds
½ cup *(125 mL)* sugar
4 egg whites, slightly beaten
3 tbsp. *(45 mL)* flour
½ tsp. *(2 mL)* vanilla

Heat the butter in a small heavy saucepan, just until it starts turning brown. Set aside.

Put the toasted ground almonds in a bowl. Stir in all the other ingredients, adding the butter last.

Put 1 heaping tsp. (7 mL) of the batter in 2½" (6 cm) muffin cups. Bake at 350°F (180°C) for 12 minutes. Watch very carefully – you are striving for perfection here.

Remove the Amandines from the oven when the edges are a nice brown. Cool for a few minutes before removing them from the pans, to avoid breakage.

Why the muffin tins for a cookie? The dough is quite runny and you want the cookies to be perfectly round.

These cookies freeze very well.

Yield: 2½ dozen cookies

Pictured on page 175.

This is a very rich cookie for very special occasions!!

Pecan Kisses

2 egg whites
2 cups *(500 mL)* brown sugar
2 tsp. *(10 mL)* vanilla
4 cups *(1 L)* coarsely chopped
   pecans

In a large bowl, with an electric mixer, beat the egg whites until stiff but not dry. Beat in the sugar 1 tbsp. (15 mL) at a time. Beat until thoroughly mixed. Stir in the vanilla and pecans.

Drop the batter by spoonfuls onto well-greased cookie sheets. Bake at 400°F(200°C) for 5 to 6 minutes. Allow to cool for 10 minutes before removing from the pans.

Yield: 30 cookies

These pecan meringue cookies have a light chewy texture – they melt in your mouth.

Danish Pastry Cookies

These popular cookies from Shirley Haworth are often called Thimble or Thumbprint Cookies because of the indent made to hold the jam.

2 cups/1 lb. *(500 mL)* butter
1 cup *(250 mL)* brown sugar
4 cups *(1 L)* flour
4 egg yolks
1 tsp. *(5 mL)* vanilla
4 egg whites, slightly beaten
2-3 cups *(500-750 mL)* finely
   chopped walnuts

red jam or jelly: raspberry,
   strawberry, red currant, etc.

In a large bowl, with an electric mixer, cream the butter and sugar until creamy. Beat in the flour, egg yolks and vanilla.

Roll the dough into balls. Roll the balls in the egg whites, then roll in the nuts.

Place the balls on greased cookie sheets. With a thimble, or the end of your finger, make a depression in each ball. Bake at 350°F (180°C) for 10 to 12 minutes. Cool.

Put ¼ to ½ tsp. (1 to 2 mL) of jam or jelly in each depression before you serve the cookies.

These cookies freeze well.

Yield: 5 dozen cookies

Pictured on page 175.

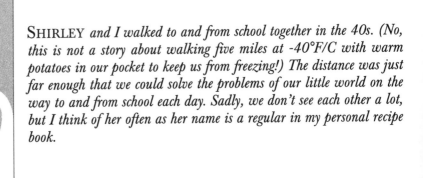

SHIRLEY *and I walked to and from school together in the 40s. (No, this is not a story about walking five miles at -40°F/C with warm potatoes in our pocket to keep us from freezing!) The distance was just far enough that we could solve the problems of our little world on the way to and from school each day. Sadly, we don't see each other a lot, but I think of her often as her name is a regular in my personal recipe book.*

Ginger Thins

1½ cups/¾ lb. *(375 mL)* butter
2 cups *(500 mL)* brown sugar
2 eggs
½ cup *(125 mL)* light molasses
3 cups *(750 mL)* flour
2 tsp. *(10 mL)* baking soda
2 tsp. *(10 mL)* cinnamon
1 tsp. *(5 mL)* cloves
2 tbsp. *(30 mL) ground* ginger

½ cup *(125 mL)* white sugar

In a large bowl, with an electric mixer, cream the butter and sugar. Beat in the eggs and molasses, followed by the dry ingredients, except for the white sugar.

Roll the dough into small balls — then roll in the white sugar. Place the sugared balls on greased cookie sheets.

Flatten the balls with a fork dipped in water. Redip frequently.

Bake at 350°F (180°C) for 10 to 12 minutes. These cookies do spread A LOT, so give them a lot of room on the cookie sheets.

Let the cookies cool a few minutes before you remove them from the cookie sheets.

These cookies freeze well.

Yield: 8 dozen

Pictured on page 175

Note: To give cookies a slightly different look — you can also flatten them with a potato masher with a grid or bars. Dip the potato masher in water to keep it from sticking to the dough.

Hazel Barber feels that her Ginger Thins are health food because they have molasses and ginger in them!! I believe her. They are also spicy and delicious!

To keep brown sugar from hardening, store it with a slice of apple in the bag or container.

To soften hardened brown sugar, place a slice of soft, fresh bread in the bag and it should soften in 2 to 3 hours.

Brown Sugar Oatmeal Cookies

Brown sugar gives Faye Noble's oatmeal cookies a slight caramel flavour. These are very good.

1 cup *(250 mL)* butter
1½ cups *(375 mL)* brown sugar
2 eggs
½ cup *(125 mL)* milk
1 tsp. *(5 mL)* vanilla
2 cups *(500 mL)* flour
½ tsp. *(2 mL)* baking soda
pinch of salt
1 tsp. *(5 mL)* baking powder
1 tsp. *(5 mL)* cinnamon
2½ cups *(625 mL)* rolled oats
1 cup *(250 mL)* raisins, chopped nuts
   OR dates (optional)

In a large bowl, with an electric mixer, cream the butter and sugar. Beat in the eggs, milk and vanilla. Beat in the dry ingredients. Stir in the raisins, nuts or dates, if using.

Drop the dough by spoonfuls onto greased cookie sheets.

Bake at 350°F (180°C) for 12 to 15 minutes.

These cookies freeze well.

Yield: 3 dozen

Pictured opposite.

Variation: Toasting or roasting the rolled oats, in a baking or cookie pan at 325°F (160°C) for 4 to 5 minutes, adds a richer caramelized flavour. Roast, stirring once or twice, just until the oats are slightly browned and fragrant.

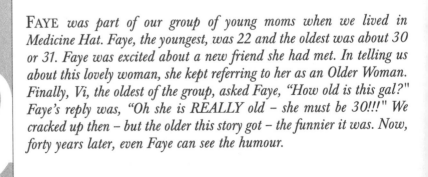

FAYE *was part of our group of young moms when we lived in Medicine Hat. Faye, the youngest, was 22 and the oldest was about 30 or 31. Faye was excited about a new friend she had met. In telling us about this lovely woman, she kept referring to her as an Older Woman. Finally, Vi, the oldest of the group, asked Faye, "How old is this gal?" Faye's reply was, "Oh she is REALLY old – she must be 30!!!" We cracked up then – but the older this story got – the funnier it was. Now, forty years later, even Faye can see the humour.*

DESSERTS & COOKIES

Oatmeal Chocolate Chip Cookies

2 cups *(500 mL)* rolled oats
1½ cups *(375 mL)* boiling water

1½ cups/¾ lb. *(375 mL)* butter
1½ cups *(375 mL)* brown sugar
2 cups *(500 mL)* flour
½ tsp. *(2 mL)* salt
1 tsp. *(5 mL)* baking soda
½ cup *(125 mL)* finely flaked
　coconut
12 oz. *(350 g)* pkg. chocolate chips

In a small bowl, pour the boiling water over the rolled oats and allow to sit until cool.

In a large bowl, with an electric mixer, cream the butter and sugar. Stir in the cooled oatmeal, flour, salt, baking soda, coconut and, last of all, the chocolate chips.

Roll the dough into small balls, about 1½" (4 cm). Place the balls on greased cookie sheets.

Flatten the balls with a fork dipped into water to keep it from sticking.

Bake at 350°F (180°C) for 10 to 12 minutes, or until lightly browned.

These cookies freeze well.

Yield: 5 dozen cookies

Pictured on page 175.

Caution: If you try to rush this, and mix everything together before the oatmeal has properly cooled, the chocolate chips will melt.

Better known at our house as O.C.C.s, this cookie has been the number one, all-time favourite in our family.

Storing chocolate properly is an important consideration. Chocolate can absorb odors from other foods or substances. It should be stored at 62 to 68°F (16 to 20°C) and at a relative humidity of no more than 50%. Condensation or storage in humid areas can cause a "sugar bloom" on the chocolate.

Milk chocolate should have a shelf life of up to one year, and dark chocolate up to 1½ years.

Crispy Oatmeal Cookies

Very simple – these thin crisp cookies are crunchy and good.

1 cup *(250 mL)* butter
1 cup *(250 mL)* sugar
2 eggs
2 cups *(500 mL)* flour
1 cup *(250 mL)* rolled oats
1 tsp. *(5 mL)* vanilla

In a large bowl, with an electric mixer, cream the butter and sugar. Beat in the eggs and vanilla.

Work in the flour and rolled oats. Drop the dough by spoonfuls onto greased cookie sheets.

Bake at 350°F (180°C) for 8 to 10 minutes.

These cookies freeze well.

Yield: 4 dozen cookies

THIS TYPE *of cookie was probably used in the lunch boxes that were prepared for Box Socials in the early days when the west was being settled. The Box Social was a way of raising money for community expenses – probably the school or church. Women would go to great lengths to fix up a box lunch that was not only delicious on the inside – but pretty on the outside. As they arrived at the dance the boxes were gathered in one area – and at lunch time (probably midnight) an auctioneer would auction the boxes to the highest bidder. The current beaus had probably been given hints as to which box they were to be bidding on, but sometime the best laid plans went awry.*

On this subject – my uncle Rolland, who is now 87, told me that at one social he thought he was bidding on his current heartthrob's box, and he ended up having lunch with an older woman, with six kids. He claims it was the best box lunch he could remember – so all was not lost.

Another experience he related was about his best friend, Shorty, who was madly in love with the current teacher. When her box came up all the young men started bidding on it. They ran it up to an unheard of price before Shorty finally procured it. At that point, Shorty had to go to all his friends (the same ones who had bid against him) and borrow a dollar from each of them to pay the purchase price. Just in passing – Shorty married the teacher.

It was all in good fun, and a way of raising a little bit of money for the community.

Spicy Hermits

½ cup *(125 mL)* butter
1 cup *(250 mL)* sugar
½ cup *(125 mL)* light molasses
½ cup *(125 mL)* warm water
1 tsp. *(5 mL)* baking soda
3 cups *(750 mL)* flour
1 tsp. *(5 mL)* cloves
1 tsp. *(5 mL)* cinnamon
pinch of salt
1 cup *(250 mL)* raisins, chopped
    dates and/or nuts

In a large bowl, with an electric mixer, cream the butter and sugar. Add the molasses and water, beating on low until the batter is smooth.

Add all of the dry ingredients, beating again until smooth.

Stir in the fruit and/or nuts.

Drop the dough by spoonfuls onto greased cookie sheets.

Bake at 350°F (180°C) for 10 to 12 minutes.

These cookies freeze well.

Yield: 5 dozen

Pictured on page 175.

I can't imagine a picnic without Mrs. Knight's Spicy Hermits!!! These chewy cookies keep very well – they taste even better after a few days storage.

MRS. KNIGHT *was not only a great cook, she was a great old gal who put on a happy face no matter how bumpy the road of life became. She worked on the theory that anything that could go wrong – would. And it did. She played the cards she was dealt and never complained – just took life as it came. Her endearing qualities were many, the most amazing being her cheerful acceptance and endurance.*

Chocolate Cheese Drops

Who can resist a chocolate cookie? Cream cheese makes these cookies a melt-in-your-mouth treat.

12 oz. *(340 g)* semisweet chocolate
2 tsp. *(10 mL)* vanilla
4 tbsp. *(60 mL)* milk

2 cups/1 lb. *(500 mL)* butter
8 oz. *(250 g)* cream cheese
3 cups *(750 mL)* sugar
2 eggs
pinch of salt
4½ cups *(1.125 L)* flour
1 tbsp. *(15 mL)* baking powder
1 cup *(250 mL)* chopped roasted
   nuts

In a small pan, gently heat the chocolate with the vanilla and milk, just to soften the chocolate.

In a large bowl, with an electric mixer, cream the butter and cream cheese until smooth. Beat in the sugar and eggs, then beat in the salt, flour and baking powder.

Stir in the nuts and then the melted chocolate.

Drop the dough by spoonfuls onto well-buttered cookie sheets.

Bake at 350°F (180°C) for 12 to 15 minutes.

These cookies freeze well.

Yield: 7 dozen cookies

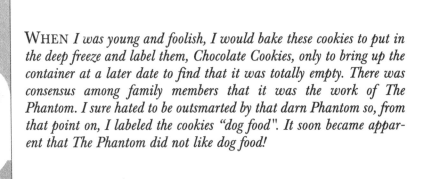

WHEN *I was young and foolish, I would bake these cookies to put in the deep freeze and label them, Chocolate Cookies, only to bring up the container at a later date to find that it was totally empty. There was consensus among family members that it was the work of The Phantom. I sure hated to be outsmarted by that darn Phantom so, from that point on, I labeled the cookies "dog food". It soon became apparent that The Phantom did not like dog food!*

Chocolate Chip Cookies

1 cup *(250 mL)* butter
½ cup *(125 mL)* white sugar
1 cup *(250 mL)* brown sugar
1 tsp. *(5 mL)* vanilla
2 eggs
1 tsp. *(5 mL)* baking soda
pinch of salt
2 cups + 2 tbsp. *(500 mL)* flour
1 cup *(250 mL)* chopped walnuts
12½ oz. *(350 g)* pkg. chocolate chips

In a large bowl, with an electric mixer, cream the butter and sugars. Beat in the vanilla and eggs, then the baking soda, salt and flour.

Stir in the walnuts and chocolate chips. Mix thoroughly.

Drop the dough by spoonfuls on well-buttered cookie sheets.

Bake at 350°F (180°C) for 12 to 15 minutes.

These cookies freeze well.

Yield: 6 dozen cookies

Pictured on page 175.

Variation: If you want to make **Chocolate Chunk Cookies**, just revert to the days before commercial chocolate chips, and coarsely chop semisweet baking chocolate into chunks.

Chocolate Chip Cookies were originally called Toll House Cookies, for the restaurant in Massachusetts where chocolate chips were "invented". Previously, cookie bakers used to chop up chocolate bars to create their own chocolate bits or chips.

CHOCOLATE CHIPS *were the first real luxury that surfaced right after the Second World War. At first it felt almost sinful when rationing was lifted from sugar and butter, BUT THEN – to be able to buy something like chocolate chips to use in baking. It was an unbelievable delight. They caught on right away!!!*

Double Chocolate Cookies

Nicole Martin and Amanda Martin, my granddaughters, like lots of chocolate. Naturally, their favourites, these soft chewy cookies, have cocoa in the batter as well as chocolate chips.

½ cup *(125 mL)* butter
¾ cup *(175 mL)* sugar
1 egg
1 tsp. *(5 mL)* vanilla
1 cup *(250 mL)* flour
½ tsp. *(2 mL)* baking soda
⅓ cup *(75 mL)* cocoa
¼ tsp. *(1 mL)* salt
½-1 cup *(125-250 mL)* chocolate chips

In a mixing bowl, with an electric mixer, cream the butter and sugar. Beat in the egg and vanilla. Beat in the flour, baking soda, cocoa and salt. Stir in the chocolate chips.

Drop the dough by spoonfuls on greased cookie sheets. Press down gently with a fork dipped in a glass of water.

Bake at 350°F (180°C) for 10 minutes.

These cookies freeze well.

Yield: 30 cookies

DOUG AND I *had our youngest granddaughters at the lake last year, and they wanted to make this recipe. We had no chocolate chips, so we went for a walk and picked up a couple of milk chocolate bars. For some strange reason Nicole and Grandpa insisted upon hiding them. (They were afraid Amanda and I might eat them – a likely possibility!) They hid the bars and went outside to spend the evening by the fire. Quietly, Amanda and I searched all the bedrooms for the bars, with no luck. We went to bed early.*

Quietly, we got up at seven the next morning and searched the main part of the house, leaving the kitchen to the last. We got to the very last cupboard, the one that held the breakfast cereal. Voila, there they were in the Corn Flakes. We quickly hid them under the egg carton in the fridge, and made pancakes for breakfast for the late risers. Eventually, we started organizing everything for the cookies, at which point I suggested that they get out the bars. Doug and Nicole did not want to disclose their secret hiding place, so they insisted Amanda and I go to the bedroom and shut the door. We were happy to do so because we were shaking so hard trying not to laugh. When we heard the roar of disbelief, Amanda and I hurried back into the kitchen to see Grandpa's face. He had been so confident that he had the perfect hiding place that he told Nikki the night before, "They won't find them here in a hundred years." We laughed so hard and long that we were hardly able to make cookies. One little giggle would get us all going again.

Peanut Butter Cookies

1 cup *(250 mL)* butter
1 cup *(250 mL)* white sugar
1 cup *(250 mL)* brown sugar
1 cup *(250 mL)* smooth or chunky peanut butter
2 eggs
2 cups *(500 mL)* flour
1 tsp. *(5 mL)* baking soda
pinch of salt

In a large bowl, with an electric mixer, cream the butter and sugars. Beat in the peanut butter and eggs. Beat in the flour, soda and salt.

Roll the dough into balls, 1" (2.5 cm) or 1½" (4 cm), and place on greased cookie sheets. Press down the balls with a fork dipped in water to keep it from sticking.

Bake at 350°F (180°C) for 10 to 12 minutes.

These cookies freeze well.

Yield: 7 dozen cookies

Pictured on page 175.

When Evelyn Lutes' family and mine were young, we considered Peanut Butter Cookies to be in the staple food group. This is Evelyn's recipe.

Peanut Butter Balls

1 cup *(250 mL)* smooth peanut butter
½ cup *(125 mL)* butter
2½ cups *(625mL)* icing sugar

8, 1 oz. *(30 g)* squares semisweet chocolate*
2 cups *(500 mL)* crushed nuts or flaked coconut

In a small bowl, mix the peanut butter, butter and icing sugar. Roll into 1" (2.5 cm) balls. Chill.

Melt the chocolate in the top of a double boiler.

Roll the peanut butter balls in chocolate, then in crushed nuts. Allow to cool. Refrigerate in an airtight container until time to serve.

These balls freeze well.

Yield: 7 dozen balls – depending how large you make the balls

These are classed as cookies, but they border on being candy. If you have a special occasion coming up – they are worth the time and effort.

* Dipping chocolate (couverture) is a higher butter-fat-content chocolate that is available at specialty stores or large supermarkets. It is formulated specially for coating truffles and candies. Try it if you want a more professional-looking product.

Chocolate Fudge

2 cups *(500 mL)* white sugar
2 cups *(500 mL)* brown sugar
½ cup *(125 mL)* corn syrup
½ cup *(125 mL)* cocoa
1 cup *(250 mL)* whipping cream
½ cup *(125 mL)* butter
1 tsp. *(5 mL)* vanilla

Fudge can be creamy smooth or laden with chopped nuts and fruit. This creamy chocolate version is delicious – we usually pour it onto a platter and eat it as soon as it is ready.

A candy thermometer is necessary for this recipe.

Put the sugars, syrup, cocoa and cream into a heavy saucepan. Heat gently. Stir gently and only occasionally – just enough to keep it from burning, until it gets to the soft-ball stage, 234°F (112°C). **(Too much stirring causes the sugar to crystallize.)**

Remove the fudge from the heat. Allow it to cool to 200°F (93°C), then stir in the butter and vanilla. Beat the fudge with a wooden spoon until it thickens.

Pour the fudge into a buttered 9" (23 cm) square pan or, if you want a thinner fudge, onto a 9 x 12" (23 x 30 cm) platter. Let it set, but cut the fudge into squares before it hardens too much. Store it in an airtight container.

No COOKBOOK *of mine would be complete without a chocolate fudge recipe. When I was little my Aunt Edith made fudge on Christmas Eve. It became a family tradition for any festive occasion. The more people on hand to help with the beating – the better. My boys were always eager to help with the fudge-making process. However, it was the wide-eyed enthusiasm of my grandchildren that made candy making a delight.*

They would come over before the holiday season, perhaps bringing a friend, and we would spend the day making different kinds of candy. A necessary part of the process was to taste as we tested and, last but not least, to scrape out the pot.

The highlight of it all, for me, was to see the joy in their eyes as they departed with the fruits of their labour, carefully packaged to take home to share with their parents.

Candy Temperature Chart

Type of Candy	Temperature	Cold Water Test
fudge	234-240°F (112-116°C)	soft ball
fondant	238-240°F (115-116°C)°	soft ball
caramels	244-248°F (118-120°C)	firm ball
taffy	250-266°F (121-130°C)	hard ball
butterscotch, toffee	290-300°F (143-150°C)	crack
brittles	300-310°F (150-154°C)	hard crack

Divinity Fudge

3 cups *(750 mL)* white sugar
1 cup *(250 mL)* corn syrup
¾ cup *(175 mL)* boiling water
2 egg whites, stiffly beaten
½ cup *(125 mL)* chopped, roasted
   almonds
1 tsp. *(5 mL)* vanilla

A candy thermometer if is necessary for this recipe.

Combine the sugar, corn syrup and boiling water in a heavy saucepan. Heat gently and stir very little. Boil to the firm-ball stage, 248°F (120°C). Cool slightly.

Beat the egg whites until stiff. Gradually beat the hot syrup into the egg whites, pouring the syrup in a thin stream. Beat until thick and creamy.

Stir in the nuts and vanilla. Pour the fudge into a buttered 9" (23 cm) square pan or onto a 9 x 12" (23 x 30 cm) platter.

Cut the cooled fudge into squares and store it in an airtight container.

This is very sweet, so cut it into small pieces. You could also try different flavourings – almond, maple, rum – they all work well.

Maple Cream

3 cups *(750 mL)* brown sugar
¼ cup *(60 mL)* maple syrup
⅔ cup *(150 mL)* evaporated milk
3 tbsp. *(45 mL)* butter
½ cup *(125 mL)* chopped walnuts
1 tsp. *(5 mL)* vanilla

A candy thermometer is necessary for this recipe.

In a heavy saucepan, combine the sugar, syrup and milk and heat gently. Stir gently until the sugar is dissolved. Simmer gently to 234°F (112°C), soft-ball stage. **Stir as little as possible – the stirring causes the sugar to crystallized in the finished product.**

Cool to 200°F (93°C) and add the butter and vanilla.

Beat the fudge with a wooden spoon until almost stiff. Stir in the nuts.

Pour the fudge into a buttered 9" (23 cm) square pan or onto a 9 x 12" (23 x 30 cm) platter.

Cut the cooled fudge into squares and store it in an airtight container.

Nuts are a delicious addition to this fudge. Maple and walnuts just seem to belong together.

Nuts are best stored in their shells because they will keep longer without their oils going rancid. If buying them shelled, choose plump, crisp nuts.

Shelled walnuts, stored in the refrigerator, in an airtight container, should keep for about 6 months. In the freezer they should keep for up to 1 year.

Taffy

3 cups *(750 mL)* brown sugar
1 cup *(250 mL)* corn syrup
1 cup *(250 mL)* butter
10 oz. *(300 mL)* can sweetened
   condensed milk

In a heavy saucepan, combine the sugar, syrup and butter and boil gently, for 5 minutes.

Stir in the sweetened condensed milk and continue boiling for 20 minutes. You must stir almost constantly as taffy burns very easily.

Pour into a buttered 9" (23 cm) square pan.

Cut the cooled taffy into squares and store it in an airtight container.

Note: Taffy or toffee is usually soft and chewy, for a crunchy version it is cooked to 310°F (154°C), hard-crack stage, on a candy thermometer.

If I were making candy this afternoon – this recipe of Adele Armstrong's would be my first choice!!

WHEN GREG *and Dan were little, I guess I didn't have enough to do, so I took piano lessons from Adele. I was not by any stretch of the imagination talented but, with Adel's superb teaching skills, I was teachable. It was great fun and now, forty-some years later, I wish I had kept it up.*

At that time, Adele was kind enough to share this taffy recipe. It was one that had been an Armstrong family favourite for a couple of generations. Thanks for sharing, Adele.

Pull Taffy

Christopher, my Grandson, loves this recipe – but hesitates to suggest making it. Pulling the taffy is what gives it the elastic, chewy consistency. Vanilla, brandy or rum flavouring may also be added.

1 cup *(250 mL)* **white sugar**
1 cup *(250 mL)* **brown sugar**
2 cups *(500 mL)* **light molasses**
¾ cup *(175 mL)* **water**

½ cup *(125 mL)* **butter**
⅛ tsp. *(0.5 mL)* **baking soda**
¼ tsp. *(1 mL)* **salt**

A candy thermometer is necessary for this recipe.

Put the sugars, molasses and water into a heavy saucepan and cook to 265°F (129°C), hard-ball stage. Cook it slowly, stirring during the latter stages of cooking to prevent it from burning.

Remove the pan from the heat and stir in the butter, baking soda and salt. Stir just enough to mix well.

Pour the taffy into a greased 9 x 12" (23 x 30 cm) pan and allow it to stand until cool enough to handle.

With well-greased hands, gather the taffy into a ball and pull, folding it over and stretching it out until it is rather firm and of a light yellow colour.

Stretch out the taffy in a long rope, cut it into pieces, and wrap it in waxed paper if it is to be stored for some time.

Store in an airtight container to keep it from absorbing moisture and getting sticky.

ONE *Saturday, when I had Christopher and Tracey for a weekend, we decided that we really should make some candy. Tracey and I voted for Chocolate Fudge. Chris wanted Pull Taffy. There was a lot of debate, and a few heated words, because Tracey and I felt that taffy took too long and was too messy – we had all the right arguments – but somehow we lost.*

When we were about halfway to the "hard-ball stage" Chris announced that he had to go to hockey practice! We screeched at him as he was going out the door – and continued it two hours later when he came back, just as we had completed pulling the taffy and wrapping it. We never, ever, admitted that the taffy was a nice change from the chocolate fudge!

Canning — Preserves & Pickles

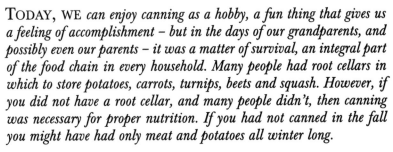

CANNING —
In the Good Old Days ‼

TODAY, WE *can enjoy canning as a hobby, a fun thing that gives us a feeling of accomplishment – but in the days of our grandparents, and possibly even our parents – it was a matter of survival, an integral part of the food chain in every household. Many people had root cellars in which to store potatoes, carrots, turnips, beets and squash. However, if you did not have a root cellar, and many people didn't, then canning was necessary for proper nutrition. If you had not canned in the fall you might have had only meat and potatoes all winter long.*

Before the canning started the gardening had to be done. This was often done in the evening, AFTER a full day of hard work.

In the summer heat the gardens matured quickly, and once the canning started vegetables ripened in rapid succession – almost daily.

The vegetables were a joy to harvest in the cool of the evening, but in the morning, in the heat of the day, the women of the household had to fire up the insatiable wood stoves and keep them hot all day. There were many trips to the wood pile, not only for the canning but for the three meals for that day. With no air conditioning, windows and doors were opened wide (if they had screens on to keep out the flies) hoping for a little movement of air.

The canners were very large oval, copper vessels that measured 12 x 27 to 14" (30 x 68 to 35 cm) high, and could accommodate up to 36 quart (1 L) jars at one time. These versatile tubs were double handled, with a lid, and were also used for heating water for the weekly baths and for washing clothes. They were so heavy that the men had to lift them going on and off the stoves.

At the end of the day, canning done, meals finished, dishes done, chores done (which for the women included washing and sanitizing the milk separator – which is another story), floors mopped up – it was time to go back to the garden to see what was ready for tomorrow!!!

Those women never complained – they even looked forward to that tomorrow.

CANNING — Procedures

Wash: Everything needs to be well washed, fruit and vegetables as well as the jars.

Blanch: Tomatoes and peaches need to be blanched. This means that you must have a large pot of boiling water – preferably with a removable basket. Put the fruit in the basket and lower it into the boiling water. Normally this only takes about 2 minutes, but try one first. Take it out of the boiling water and drop it into cold water. The skin should slip right off. If it does not slip off easily – leave it another minute or so. (It could also mean that the fruit is still green.)

Packing: Packing the fruit, meat or whatever is fairly simple. Fill the jar only to the base of the neck. Put in salt, if required, or syrup, if required, depending on what you are canning.

Salt: The salt that is used in canning MUST be Coarse Pickling Salt. Any other kind will turn your canned produce or meats a murky colour.

Putting on lids: This is the most important part of canning. It must be done correctly or the jars will not seal. Put the **new** snap-on flat lids in a pan of water and bring the water to a boil. Have the jars full. Have a dish with clean water nearby. Take a clean cloth and wipe the rim of the jar. Dip a finger into the clean water and run the finger around the rim – looking for either a chip in the glass (if you find a chipped jar – discard it) or a bit of food stuck on the lip. The lip must be absolutely clean. Now, lift a lid out of the hot water, place it on the jar and put on the screw top, firmly – but not too firm.

Water Bath: In the canner is a jar rack, usually for 7 jars. As you put the lids on the jars, place them in the jar rack in the canner. When all 7 jars are in the rack, fill the canner with warm water up to the top of the jars. Turn on the heat and bring to a boil. Time the processing from the time the boil starts – not from when you put the jars in the canner. Once it starts to boil, turn down the heat – so that it just barely boils.

After the boiling time is complete, take the jars out of the water to cool. As the jars cool the lids will pop. They must pop inward (become concave) or the jars are not sealed.

Note: When you open a canned jar, the lid must pop – if it doesn't – don't eat the contents.

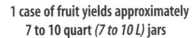

Canned Fruit

Canning fruit can be fun or a nightmare – I hope you try it and have fun doing it. The rewards are great!!! Remember – every lid should pop inward as the jars cool. These pops are music to the ears of those doing the canning.

1 case of fruit yields approximately 7 to 10 quart *(7 to 10 L)* jars

select choice ripe fruit: peaches (freestone), pears, plums or apricots

select the syrup you prefer

Syrups:

Light: 2 cups *(500 mL)* of sugar to 4 cups *(1 L)* of water

Medium: 3 cups *(750 mL)* sugar to 4 cups *(1 L)* water

Heavy: 4 cups *(1 L)* of sugar to 4 cups *(1 L)* of water

quart jars *(1 L)*, wide mouth, with screw tops and new snap-on metal lids

Read the canning notes on page 191.

Decide which syrup you want and how much syrup you will need.

I prefer the heavy syrup so I generally start with 10 cups (2.5 L) of sugar and 10 cups (2.5 L) of water. Bring the syrup to a boil and set it aside.

Prepare the fruit. (That means take the skins off, if necessary, and/or remove the pits or, as in the case of peaches, both.

When buying peaches, make sure they are "freestone" or you will never "can" again!!! Blanch the peaches to remove the skins, cut the peaches in half and discard the pits.

Put the peach halves or other fruit in the jars – fill with hot syrup and put on the lids.

Place the filled sealed jars in a water bath for 30 to 40 minutes. Remember to time from when the water first starts to boil.

Take the jars out of the water bath and allow them to cool. Every lid should pop as the jars cool.

Note: If you are canning plums or apricots, simply cut them in half and take out the pits. Proceed as for the peaches. Pears you must peel and core.

Canned Tomatoes

20 lbs. *(10 kg)* of fresh tomatoes yield 10 quarts *(10 L)* of canned tomatoes

Per Quart:
1 tsp. *(5 mL)* pickling salt
1 tsp. *(5 mL)* sugar

quart jars, use wide-mouth jars with screw tops and new metal snap-on lids

Read the canning notes on page 191.

Wash the tomatoes and blanch them, slipping the skins off. Put the tomatoes in the waiting jars, filling to 1" (2.5 cm) from the top. Add 1 tsp. (5 mL) salt and 1 tsp. (5 mL) sugar per quart (1 L) jar.

Bring the snap-on lids to a boil. Clean the tops of the jars with clean, clear water, then dip a finger in clean water and run it around the rim of the jar to ensure there are no chips.

Put the lids on the jars and place the jars in the water bath. Boil gently for 30 minutes. (Remember to time from the first boil – not from the time in the water bath.)

Take the jars out of water bath and let cool. Every lid should pop as the jars cool.

This is Granny Olsen's recipe. I have used it for 50 years. Tomatoes are called for in so many recipes, and they are the easiest to can. Tomatoes are just about the last garden produce canned in the fall. Buy field tomatoes if you can. They should be large and ripe, large – because they are less work – ripe for the best flavour.

Vine-ripened tomatoes are the most flavourful, and succulent. Canning your own produce allows you to take advantage of tomatoes at the peak of their flavour.

If you are growing tomatoes for canning, choose determinate tomato plants as they flower and set all of their fruit in a specific time period.

Canned Meat, Poultry or Fish

Granny Olsen's recipe for canning meat and fish is another one that I have used for over 50 years. Doug is an avid fisherman, and I always have home-canned salmon on hand.

Approximate amount of meat per pint (500 mL) jar:
2 lbs. *(1 kg)* chicken, per jar
2 lbs. *(1 kg)* beef, per jar
2½ lbs. *(1.25 kg)* pork loin per jar
1 lb. *(500 g)* salmon per jar

Per pint (500 mL) jar:
¾ tsp. *(3 mL)* pickling salt

For Chicken: Use only legs, thighs and boned breasts (Use the necks and backs for making soup stock.)

For Beef: Use the round or rump, cutting pieces about the size of the jar. Cut with the grain.

For Pork: Use the loin, and cut pieces about the size of the jar. Cut with the grain.

Read the canning notes on page 191.

Use sterilized pint (500 mL) jars with straight sides, wide mouths and screw tops. Use new metal snap-on lids. Leave the lids in the hot water, so they are hot and ready when you need them.

Note: For the salmon use the regular salmon jars which are 3" (8 cm) tall. They also have wide mouths, and snap-on lids.

Pack the meat into the jars, leaving 1" (2.5 cm) headspace. Add ¾ tsp. (2 cm) pickling salt to each jar. With clean, clear water and a clean cloth, wipe off the jar top to clean away any bits or pieces that may have stuck while you were packing them.

Dip a finger in clean water and run it around the rim as a second check. Take the lids out of the hot water and place them on very carefully.

Pack the jars into the canner. Cover the jars with warm water and bring the water to a boil.* Start timing from the time the water boils. Keep at a soft boil for 3 hours.

Remove the jars carefully from the canner and allow them to cool. The lids should all pop as the jars cool. If one doesn't – simply use it right away.

CAUTION: Cooking meat and fish the proper, required time is important to avoid botulism!

* When adding water to the canner to keep the level up, make sure it is boiling water or your timing will not be accurate.

Apple Butter

8 cups *(2 L)* crabapple pulp

8 cups *(2 L)* sugar
2 tsp. *(10 mL)* cinnamon
½ tsp. *(2 mL)* cloves

6 pint *(500 mL)* jelly jars with screw tops and new snap-on lids

Read the canning notes on page 191.

Wash the crabapples, removing the stems and the blossom ends. Place the crabapples in a large pot; just barely cover with water and simmer until they turn to mush. Stir often, scraping the bottom to make sure the pulp doesn't stick. Cool.

Press the pulp through a food mill, saving the pulp and discarding the seed residue.

Measure 8 cups (2 L) of pulp into a large 2-quart (2 L) stainless steel pot. Bring to a boil, stirring constantly with a flat-tipped wooden spoon. Boil for 5 minutes, then stir in the sugar, cinnamon and cloves. Bring to a boil again for about 5 minutes.

Do a gel test – spoon 1 tbsp. (15 mL) of the Apple Butter onto a cool plate and place it in the freezer compartment of the refrigerator for a couple of minutes. If it gels or thickens it is ready to bottle.

Bottle and seal. Water bath processing is not necessary with this recipe, but the lids should all pop as the jars cool.

Yield: approximately 6 pint (500 mL) jars

Aunt Edith's Apple Butter recipe is wonderful. Use it like jam on toast or muffins. Choose the crabapples carefully. They must be the little bright red tart crabs for the best flavour and colour.

Apricot Jam

Kay Martin, my sister-in-law, made luscious Apricot Jam. Chop the apricots coarsely if you like a jam with lots of fruit bits or purée them if you prefer a smooth-textured jam.

4 cups *(1 L)* apricot pulp*
4 tbsp. *(60 mL)* fresh lemon juice
4 tbsp. *(60 mL)* frozen orange juice concentrate
2, 14 oz. *(398 mL)* cans crushed pineapple
6 cups *(1.5 L)* sugar

6 to 8 pint *(500 mL)* jars with screw tops and new snap-on lids

Read the canning notes on page 191.

Wash and pit the apricots. Chop them or process in a food processor or blender.

Combine the fruit pulp, lemon juice, orange juice and crushed pineapple in a stainless steel 2-quart (2 L) saucepan. Bring it to a boil, stirring constantly to keep the fruit from sticking to the bottom. Simmer for 15 minutes.

Add the sugar. Return to a boil and simmer until the jam seems to thicken.

To do a gel test, place 1 tbsp. 15 mL) of jam on a cool saucer and place it in the freezer for a couple of minutes. If it thickens or gels, it is ready to bottle.

Bottle while hot and seal. Water bath processing is not necessary with jam, but the lids should all pop as the jars cool.

Yield: 6 to 8 pint (500 mL) jars

* 1 lb. (500 g) of apricots averages 1½ cups (375 mL) of pulp

When you are canning jelly, it has always been a problem as to how to strain the juice through a bag to drip into a container. Many times I looked for a Sky Hook to hold up the bag. WELL, I read something the other day that will solve that problem. Take an ordinary kitchen stool, one that does not have a back on it, turn it upside down and then you have the rungs and the legs onto which you can tie the jelly bag. Good tip.

Raspberry Jam (Freezer)

3 cups *(750 mL)* crushed raspberries
5¼ cups *(1.3 L)* sugar
¾ cup *(175 mL)* water
2 oz. *(57 g)* box Certo crystals

plastic freezer containers

The main thing here – is that measurements must be exact, the sugar must be dissolved and the recipe cannot be doubled.

Wash the raspberries and mash them. Place the raspberries in a large bowl. Add the sugar and let stand until the sugar is completely dissolved.

Combine the water and Certo. Bring to a boil for at least 1 minute, stirring constantly. Pour the Certo into the fruit and stir for 3 more minutes.

Put the jam into the containers and allow to remain at room temperature until it has set, 24 hours. Store in the freezer.

Raspberry Jam is a staple at our house. This freezer jam has a very distinctive fresh fruit flavour.

MY MOM'S *best friend, Eileen Choiniere, had a stroke in her seventies. She was wheelchair bound, could not speak. She lived in a nursing home – but she still enjoyed socializing. Once a month we would pick her up to share the family Sunday brunch. On one such occasion, with about twelve of us sitting around the dining room table, Wendy volunteered to help Mrs. C. She gave her a generous dollop of raspberry jam on her waffle. Mrs. C. started eating with great enthusiasm.*

I was in the kitchen tending the waffle iron when, suddenly, there was total silence in the dining room. One of the boys croaked, "MOM". When I stepped into the dining room, Mrs. C. had removed her dentures, covered with raspberry seeds, and had set them in the middle of the table. Total Silence! No one moved! Every eye was on the dentures! My grandchildren's eyes were as big as saucers!

With the speed of light, Wendy whisked away the offending waffle, replacing it with one smothered with maple syrup, while I quickly cleaned and replaced the dentures. Conversation resumed and breakfast continued as if nothing happened. Eileen often poked fun at herself. I wish she could have told this story herself at a cocktail party – it would have been a winner. As it is, twenty some years later, on Sunday mornings when we pass the raspberry jam, we think of that dear lady, and we smile.

Orange Marmalade

Allison Courtney uses very thin lemon slices to add extra tang and texture to her whole-orange marmalade.

1 lb. *(500 g)* oranges
2 cups *(500 mL)* water
1 lemon, thinly sliced
2 lbs. *(1 kg)* sugar

jelly jars with screw tops and new snap-on lids

Read the canning notes on page 191.

Buy oranges with very thin skins as you are using the whole orange. The thick-skinned oranges have a white spongy layer, called pith, between the orange and the skin – and it is bitter!

Cut the oranges in halves or quarters and remove the pips (seeds). Save the pips. Remove the skins and save. Remove the pith and discard it.

Put the orange pulp and skin into a food processor and chop finely. Put the chopped orange into a stainless steel saucepan and cover with the water. Tie the pips into a cloth and let them soak also. (Use the lemon pips too.) This should sit for at least 24 hours.

Remove the pips. Bring the orange mixture to a boil and let it simmer for 1 hour. Add the lemon slices and simmer for half an hour. Add the sugar and simmer for 1 more hour.

To test to see if it is going to gel, put a little of the marmalade on a saucer and put it in the deep freeze just long enough to cool it off.

Continue to cook the marmalade until it is thickened. Put it in jars and seal.

Water bath processing is not necessary with this recipe, but the lids should all pop as the jars cool.

Yield: approximately 4 pint (4 x 500 mL) jars

I was always grateful for ALLISON*'s sense of humour. It's a valuable trait in a next-door neighbour. One evening when we had to go out for a couple of hours, Greg and Dan had a couple of friends in. They proceeded to make fudge (without permission) and hot dogs. When the fudge was just about finished, they discovered that they had mistakenly grabbed the pickling salt instead of the sugar. At that point, to get rid of the evidence, they threw everything, fudge, hot dogs and all, over the fence into Allison's backyard. The next day she put her two young children out in the backyard to play and they found this wonderful treasure. They ate the hot dogs – dirt and all. They passed on the fudge!*

Hot Tamale Salsa/Chutney

15 large ripe tomatoes
6 large onions
4 large peaches
4 pears
4 apples
12 chili peppers
3 cups *(750 mL)* diced celery
3 cups *(750 mL)* brown sugar
1 tbsp. *(15 mL)* pickling salt
3 tbsp. *(45 mL)* pickling spice in a bag
1½ cups *(375 mL)* Heinz pickling vinegar
½ tsp. *(2 mL)* cayenne, more if you like it zingy

pickle jars with screw tops and new snap-on lids

Read the canning notes on page 191.

Chop all of the ingredients and put them in a heavy stainless steel pot (NOT aluminum).

Simmer for a very long time, until it thickens, about 2 hours. Stir occasionally and watch carefully so that it does not burn on the bottom.

Fill the jars and seal. Place the jars in the water bath and boil gently for 20 minutes – timing from when the water starts to boil.

Take the jars out of the water bath and let them cool. Every lid should pop as the jars cool.

Yield: approximately 10 pint (500 mL) jars

This has a little zing to it! Try it with corn chips. This salsa/chutney is very versatile in that it can be used on any kind of meat, sandwich or as a salsa.

THERE *are many variations to this recipe, but the basic ingredient is tomatoes. Growing up in Medicine Hat, every gardener had a surplus of tomatoes by fall so this was one way to put them to good use. Everyone had their own version, each one a little different from the other, but all of them good.*

Pickled Beets

Polly Eckart, my aunt Edith's sister-in-law, gave me this wonderful recipe. Polly lives alone at the age of 90 – she keeps a tidy house, tends to her garden, is sharp as a tack and makes wonderful Pickled Beets.

beets, cooked, skinned and sliced

Brine ratio:
2 cups *(500 mL)* sugar
2 cups *(500 mL)* water
2 cups *(500 mL)* Heinz pickling
  vinegar

Spice-in-a-bag ratio:
1 tsp. *(5 mL)* allspice berries
1 tbsp. *(15 mL)* broken cinnamon
  sticks
1 tsp. *(5 mL)* whole cloves
1 lemon, very thinly sliced

wide-mouth jars with screw caps
  and new snap-on lids

Read the canning notes on page 191.

Scrub the beets very well. Cook the beets in salted water until tender, about 20 minutes for baby beets, 30 minutes for medium beets and 50 minutes for large beets.

Skin and slice the beets and pack them into the clean jars.

While the beets are cooking, prepare the brine. Combine the brine ingredients in a stainless steel pot. Tie the spices in a cloth to be removed later. Add them to the brine. Simmer long enough for the spice flavour to be apparent, about 20 to 30 minutes. (The amount of brine you must prepare is relative to how many beets you have.)

Remove the spice bag.

Pack the beets in clean jars and pour the brine over the beets. Wipe off the mouth of each jar with a clean cloth and water; run a finger around the rim. Seal the jars.

Place the jars in a water bath and boil gently for 20 minutes – timing from when the water starts to boil.

Remove the jars and cool. Every lid should pop as the jars cool.

Yield: 1 lb. (500 g) of beets yields approximately 1 pint (500 mL) of pickles

Sauerkraut in a Jar

shredded cabbage, enough to fit into a 2-quart *(2 L)* jar

Per quart Jar:
1 tbsp. *(15 mL)* pickling salt
1 tsp. *(5 mL)* sugar
2 tbsp. *(30 mL)* vinegar
boiling water

1 glass of wine*

wide-mouth jars with screw caps and new snap-on lids

Read the canning notes on page 191.

Sterilize a 2-quart (2 L) jar or jars and a metal snap-on lid(s). Leave the lid(s) in the boiling water.

Pack the cabbage loosely into the jar(s). Add pickling salt, sugar and vinegar. Pour boiling water into the jar(s) to 1" (2.5 cm) from the top.

Wipe the mouth of the jar(s) and put the metal snap-on lid(s) in place, followed by the screw top(s).

Let the sealed jar(s) stand in a cool dark place until the cabbage ferments and is sour, about 3 to 4 weeks.

*OH – THE WINE? You guessed it – Doreen recommends that you put 1 tbsp. (15 mL) into the jar and drink the rest while you are working in the kitchen!!

Doreen Barkley's homemade sauerkraut is very much better than the commercially canned or bottled variety. Try it with German, Polish or Alsatian sausages.

LETTING THE *cabbage ferment in jars is a more socially acceptable method than the earlier methods in which a large stoneware crock was filled with layers of cabbage and pickling salt. Topped with a weighted plate, the cabbage was left to ferment in a cool, dark place for about 3 weeks. The flavour was wonderful, but the aroma could be pervasive!*

Dill Pickles

A good dill pickle makes any sandwich seem like a banquet. Edith and Polly Eckart's recipe makes VERY good dill pickles

10 lbs. *(4.5 kg)* small cucumbers
20 sprays of fresh dill (a whole head and about 12" *(30 cm)* of the stem for both the bottom and top of each jar)

Per quart jar:
1 tbsp. *(15 mL)* coarse pickling salt
1 tbsp. *(15 mL)* brown sugar
1 garlic clove, more if you like
1 slice of onion
1 bay leaf
1 red chili pepper

Brine:
4 cups *(1 L)* water
1 cup *(250 mL)* Heinz pickling vinegar

quart jars with screw tops and new snap-on lids

Read the canning notes on page 191.

Wash the cucumbers and cut off the blossom end. Put 1 spray of dill in the bottom of each jar. Pack the cucumbers into the jars. Putting a spray of dill in the top of each jar.

Add the pickling salt, brown sugar, garlic, onion, bay leaf, alum and red chili pepper.

Combine the water and vinegar and bring to a boil. Pour over the cucumbers. Seal the jars.

Place the jars in a water bath and bring to a gentle boil until the pickles turn colour, no longer. Remove from the bath and let cool. Every lid should pop as the jars cool.

Yield: 10 quarts (10 L)

EDITH AND POLLY *never made a bad pickle. We used to think that maybe they had special water in Maple Creek, but we finally came to the realization that they not only knew what they were doing – they were experts!*

Index

Share *My Goose is Cooked* with a friend

My Goose is Cooked – Five Generations of Home Cooking is $19.95 per book plus
$4.00 (total order) for shipping and handling.

My Goose is Cooked _____ number of books ....x $19.95 = $ _____
Shipping and handling charge.. = $ ___4.00___
Subtotal .... = $ _____
In Canada add 7% GST OR 15% HST where applicable .... = $ _____
Total enclosed... = $ _____

U.S. and international orders payable in U.S. funds./Price is subject to change.

NAME: _____

STREET: _____

CITY: _____   PROV./STATE _____

COUNTRY: _____   POSTAL CODE/ZIP _____

TELEPHONE: _____   FAX: _____

Please make cheque or money order payable to: Marfac Industries Ltd.
                                                    38 Patterson Drive S.W.
            Fax: (403) 242-7985   Calgary, Alberta
            E-mail: oneym@telusplanet.net   Canada   T3H 2B7

For fundraising or volume purchase prices, contact *Marfac Industries Ltd.*
Please allow 3-4 weeks for delivery.

Share *My Goose is Cooked* with a friend

My Goose is Cooked – Five Generations of Home Cooking is $19.95 per book plus
$4.00 (total order) for shipping and handling.

My Goose is Cooked _____ number of books ....x $19.95 = $ _____
Shipping and handling charge.. = $ ___4.00___
Subtotal .... = $ _____
In Canada add 7% GST OR 15% HST where applicable .... = $ _____
Total enclosed... = $ _____

U.S. and international orders payable in U.S. funds./Price is subject to change.

NAME: _____

STREET: _____

CITY: _____   PROV./STATE _____

COUNTRY: _____   POSTAL CODE/ZIP _____

TELEPHONE: _____   FAX: _____

Please make cheque or money order payable to: Marfac Industries Ltd.
                                                    38 Patterson Drive S.W.
            Fax: (403) 242-7985   Calgary, Alberta
            E-mail: oneym@telusplanet.net   Canada   T3H 2B7

For fundraising or volume purchase prices, contact *Marfac Industries Ltd.*
Please allow 3-4 weeks for delivery.